The

Unshakable

Leader

Thriving in Leadership Crucibles!

BSK Publishing

ISBN - Paperback: 978-1-998585-23-6

DISCLAIMER

The content provided in this book is designed to provide helpful information on the subjects discussed. This book is not meant to be used, nor should it be used, to diagnose or treat any medical condition. The claims in this book are theoretical and to be used for illustrative purposes only. The publisher and the authors are not responsible for any actions you take or do not take as a result of reading this book and are not liable for any damages or negative consequences from action or inaction to any person reading or following the information in this book. References are provided for informational purposes only and do not constitute endorsement of any websites or other sources. Readers should also be aware that the websites listed in this book may change or become obsolete.

Book Dedication page information

For: My Exceptional First Lady "my Chick" Carol and Elegant Children: Madison, Morgan, Unathi, Nkosi Jr, MercyGrace. My nieces Panashe, Lulu and nephews Tinotenda, Chimba and Twalu. You are the leaders the world has been waiting for. You are the Unshakable Leaders with resilience to lead whilst bleeding. Welcome to the HOW of your WHY!

For: ALL with the special calling to "Bleedership". Those who are to lead whilst bleeding: seasoned, middle and emerging leaders.

For: ALL who gave me permission to lead them through these many years and ALL who allowed me to experience the lessons through the blessing called pain.

As a leader always remember that: Problems are not the problem. Psychiatrist Theodore Isaac Rubin once said, "The problem is not that there are problems. The problem is expecting otherwise and thinking that having problems is a problem."

If problems were the reason why a leader should move on, Moses would have never gotten Israel out of Egypt, much less across the Red Sea. Joshua would have never made it any further than Ai. Gideon would have continued working on the threshing floor and never defeated the Midianites. David would have stayed with the sheep and never glorified God by killing Goliath. Daniel would have never risen to godly prominence in the Babylonian empire or experienced God as the Lion tamer He is. Shadrach, Meshach and Abednego would have never attended "He won't put the fire out" class where they met the Fourth Man in the midst of the burning furnace. Jeremiah would have stopped prophesying. Peter would have stopped preaching and gone back to fishing. Stephen would have been lost to world history than celebrated as a hero of the early Church. Paul would have been stuck to tent making and never taken a missionary journey. Jesus would have never died on the cross.

Today we need leaders who don't lack perseverance and resilience. We need leaders with gutsy tenacity that battles through what others walk around, the dedication that has always been the difference between results and regrets. We need leaders today who will stick with stuff. We need leaders with a tough hide and a tender heart. We need leaders who will endure knowing that the value is always greater than the cost. We need leaders who are UNSHAKABLE and who survive leadership crucibles.

#ProgressOnPurpose
#PushTheKingdom

Table of Content

The Leadership Journey: Navigating Challenges and Opportunities

Overview of Modern Leadership Complexities and Their Importance

In today's fast-paced and interconnected world, the role of a leader transcends traditional boundaries and constantly evolves to accommodate new challenges, making understanding these complexities not just beneficial but essential for any leader who wishes to remain effective and relevant in their field; indeed, the ability to grasp and navigate these complexities distinguishes exceptional leaders from the merely competent ones. As leaders, especially those who hold their faith dear, you recognize that the principles guiding you are rooted deeply in values that go beyond mere management techniques or strategies, intertwining moral guidance with professional responsibilities, leading to a leadership path that is unique and profoundly impactful if understood and implemented with wisdom and care, a journey that not only tests your abilities but also enriches your spiritual and professional growth extensively.

By embracing this book and the concepts it explores, you are setting yourself on a path to deeper understanding and more effective leadership. The complexities of modern leadership involve a blend of technological know-how, emotional intelligence, and an ability to foresee and mitigate challenges before they become obstructions, skills that are immensely beneficial in a world that values quick adaptation and decisiveness. Moreover, as you engage with these concepts, your role as a leader will start to reflect not only your professional acumen but also your spiritual depth, creating a holistic model of leadership that serves as a beacon for others within your organization and community.

Congratulations on Taking Action to Improve Leadership Skills

Taking this step towards enhancing your leadership skills marks a significant milestone in your professional journey and speaks to your commitment to not just personal but communal growth; it's a decision that positions you as a proactive leader, eager to foster an environment of continuous improvement and innovation within your sphere of influence. This proactive approach is particularly commendable as it requires humility—a willingness to acknowledge that there is always room for growth and improvement, no matter how experienced or successful one might be, which aligns beautifully with the principles most faith-based leaders cherish, emphasizing growth and improvement not just in one's self but also in one's service to others.

Your decision to engage with this material, therefore, is not just about personal development but about preparing yourself to uplift those around you, fostering a community or organization that thrives on mutual respect, shared goals, and a collective striving towards excellence. This step, while challenging, is incredibly rewarding and sets a foundation for transformative results that will resonate not only within the confines of your immediate professional relationships but also extend into the broader community, enhancing your ability to lead with conviction and compassion.

Motivation to Engage Deeply with the Material for Personal and Professional Growth

Engaging deeply with the material presented in this book is an investment in your future—one that promises substantial returns in the form of enhanced leadership capabilities and deeper personal insights; indeed, the more you invest in understanding the nuances and strategies discussed, the greater your ability to apply them effectively in your daily responsibilities, transforming challenges into opportunities for growth and learning. This deep engagement is encouraged throughout the book through practical examples, reflective questions, and actionable steps that help bridge the gap between theory and practice, ensuring that the insights you gain are not just theoretical but readily applicable in various scenarios you might face as a leader.

This engagement is not merely academic but a deeply personal process that challenges you to reflect on your values, biases, and aspirations, aligning them with the leadership strategies discussed, thereby fostering not only professional growth but personal enlightenment. As you journey through each chapter, the encouragement to apply what you learn to real-life situations helps solidify your understanding and appreciation of effective leadership, making the learning process both comprehensive and deeply transformative.

Empowerment to Apply the Book's Insights for Transformative Results

The ultimate goal of this book is to empower you, the reader, to translate the insights and strategies discussed into transformative actions that significantly enhance your leadership effectiveness; this empowerment is achieved through a careful blend of inspirational narratives, practical strategies, and reflective exercises that encourage not just understanding but action. The transformative results promised by this book are not just improvements in efficiency or productivity but profound changes in how you perceive leadership and your role as a leader, changes that are expected to ripple outwards, affecting every aspect of your professional and personal interactions.

As you apply these insights, you will begin to notice a shift in how you approach decision-making, conflict resolution, and strategic planning, becoming more intuitive, empathetic, and effective, qualities that define great leaders. Moreover, the emphasis on faith-based principles like integrity, justice, and compassion throughout the book ensures that the transformation you experience is not just professional but also spiritual, providing a comprehensive overhaul of your approach to leadership, making you not just a better leader but a profound influencer in your faith community and beyond.

My Story: Years of Leadership Insights

In my journey through various leadership roles that spanned over two and a half decades, I have encountered a multitude of challenges and experiences that have shaped my approach to effective leadership, an approach deeply rooted in faith and guided by unwavering principles that have not only helped me personally but also enabled me to lead others towards growth and success. Starting as a young leader, the responsibility felt immense, with every decision seeming like it could make or break not just my career but also impact those I was leading; through these early stages, I learned the critical importance of making decisions guided not just by short-term outcomes but by long-term values and ethics which are integral when you believe in leading a life that aligns with godly principles.

As I progressed in my career, taking on more complex roles, from managing small responsibilities to leading large responsibilities, the challenges grew in complexity and scale, presenting me with scenarios that tested my resolve, patience, and ability to stay true to my faith and values in decision-making processes. It was during these times that I realized leadership isn't just about making decisions or guiding others; it's about being a beacon of hope and morale when the waters are murky, it's about standing firm in your beliefs while being open to learning and adapting from every situation you encounter.

I have had my fair share of leadership crucibles. Moments meant and sometimes intended to break and destroy my passion to lead but God turned them into a movement of empowerment and mentoring those who are called to lead while bleeding. It's true if you accept the call to leadership you must be willing to be misunderstood, criticized, opposed, accused, and even rejected and whilst you have no control on all these, you have a choice on HOW you respond. Thus the birth of this book- The Unshakable Leader!

Transforming these challenges into opportunities for growth has been a pivotal part of my leadership journey. Each difficult situation provided a unique chance to refine my approach, whether it was dealing with a failing project, managing conflicts within the team, or facing fiscal uncertainties; these experiences taught me the invaluable lesson that every challenge carries with it a seed of equivalent or greater benefit, a concept that is easier to understand when one sees their leadership role as a service to others and to God. The lessons learned from such experiences are what I consider the backbone of true leadership—having the courage to face adversity with grace, the wisdom to extract learning from every outcome, and the faith to believe that every step taken in righteousness leads to greater good.

> *This aspect of leadership, focusing on people rather than just processes, has been both the most challenging and the most rewarding part of my career, as it aligns closely with my core belief that every individual is unique and valuable in the eyes of God.*

Moreover, navigating complex leadership situations has imbued me with a deep understanding of the human element in leadership. Recognizing the individual strengths and weaknesses within my team, aligning them with the organization's mission, and leading by example has always been at the heart of my leadership practice. It is through these practices that I have not only been able to lead teams to achieve exemplary results but also to foster environments where each member feels valued and motivated to contribute their best, in alignment with the collective goals and values we share.

In conclusion, the many years of my leadership journey have been filled with both trials and triumphs, each teaching me valuable lessons about the essence of true leadership. The insights I've gained are not merely professional but deeply personal, ingrained in a life led by faith and a commitment to serve according to the principles that uphold integrity, compassion, and perseverance. These are the lessons and experiences I aim to share with you, hopeful that they will offer guidance, inspire faith-based leadership, and provide practical strategies that you can apply in your own roles. It is with a humble heart that I invite you to delve deeper into this narrative, eager to explore together how faith and leadership intertwine to create a legacy of positive impact and enduring success.

Transformative Leadership: What You'll Learn and Why It Matters

Leaders serve as the backbone of any organization, community, or nation, and their effectiveness directly influences the lives and futures of many; hence, understanding the profound impact a leader can have is the first step toward significant personal and organizational change, which is precisely what this book aims to equip you with. The concepts and strategies discussed here are designed not just as theoretical knowledge, but as practical tools that you, as a leader who believes in divine power and guiding principles, can apply to ensure not only the success of your endeavors but also the betterment of those under your leadership. It matters not only that you lead but how you lead, and that's where the transformative power of the insights within this book comes into play, offering you a pathway to not just lead, but to inspire, motivate, and uplift.

The insights provided here go beyond conventional wisdom found in typical leadership manuals; they delve deeply into the core of what makes a leader truly effective in today's fast-paced, complex world, where ethical dilemmas and moral responsibilities intersect more frequently with day-to-day operations.

> *By the end of this book, you will have learned unique, actionable strategies that are directly applicable to your daily leadership practice—these are strategies that have been refined through years of real-world experience combined with spiritual and ethical considerations that align with your beliefs as a leader who seeks guidance and wisdom from faith.*

This is crucial because, in the contemporary setting, leaders are expected not just to manage but to inspire and to steward not only business goals but also the collective moral compass of their organizations.

Moreover, you will find that each chapter of this book addresses a specific aspect of leadership—from decision-making under pressure to fostering an inclusive, motivating workplace environment—thus ensuring that you have a holistic understanding of what effective leadership really entails.

> *By providing you with a comprehensive view of various leadership challenges and how to approach them, this book does not just aim to inform but to transform, equipping you with the necessary tools to enhance your personal effectiveness and, by extension, the performance of your organization.*

The importance of this cannot be overstated, as the ripple effects of transformative leadership can lead to enhanced follower satisfaction, stronger organizational cultures, and ultimately, sustained success and growth.

Furthermore, the detailed exploration of these concepts throughout the book ensures that you are not just reading about theoretical models but are being provided with clear, easy-to-understand, and implementable steps that you can take to apply these models in your everyday leadership scenarios. This approach is particularly important because it ensures that the learning is not passive but actively engages you in thinking critically about how you can make real changes in your leadership style and strategy. This engagement is crucial for the learning to truly take root and for the lessons of the book to translate into tangible improvements in your leadership and the wellbeing of those you lead.

In conclusion, the detailed and actionable knowledge shared in this book is crucial for any leader who believes in the power of faith and the importance of ethical leadership. The lessons contained herein are designed to challenge you to think deeply about your role and how you can use your faith and your leadership position to make a positive impact on the world. The strategies and insights are not only about leading more effectively in a traditional sense but about transforming the very essence of what it means to be a leader in today's complex world, making it imperative for you as a reader not just to absorb the information, but to act on it, to implement it, and to allow it to transform your approach to leadership.

Chapter Overview: Leadership Lessons and Their Applications

In this book, we have diligently crafted each chapter to address specific leadership challenges that you, as a leader who holds faith close, may encounter on your journey; these are not just ordinary challenges, but pivotal moments that can either forge your path towards significant achievements or lead you into common pitfalls that many leaders might not even recognize until they are entangled within them, and this overview aims to prepare your heart and mind for the rich journey ahead, laying out what each chapter entails and the unique insights you will gain.

Starting from the very first chapter, we delve into the essentials of forming a vision that aligns with your values as a faithful leader, discussing not just the importance of having a vision, but also providing step-by-step guidance on how to cultivate and refine this vision so it resonates deeply not only within your own heart but also within the hearts of those you lead; this chapter will equip you with practical tools to articulate your vision in a way that is clear and compelling, ensuring that it acts as a north star for both your decision-making processes and for inspiring your team.

Moving forward, the subsequent chapter focuses on the art of making wise decisions, a critical aspect of leadership that requires not only keen intuition but also a structured approach to evaluating options and outcomes; here, we break down the decision-making process into manageable parts, offering you a framework that you can apply in various scenarios, whether it be day-to-day choices or major strategic decisions, and each step is explained in such detail that you will feel confident in your ability to choose wisely, guided by both your faith and the best practices in leadership.

Further, we explore the challenges of communication, where many leaders often stumble, not realizing the impact of their words or the frequency of their interactions; in this chapter, I'll take you through the nuances of effective communication, emphasizing the role of active listening, the power of asking the right questions, and the importance of timely and transparent communication practices that build trust and encourage open dialogue, arming you with the skills to not just speak but to truly connect with your team and stakeholders.

Moreover, a chapter is dedicated to the delicate balance of leading with empathy while maintaining the necessary authority and discipline required to guide a team towards excellence; this segment offers a deep dive into understanding emotional intelligence and its critical application in leadership roles, providing actionable advice on how to nurture an empathetic workplace that still adheres to high standards of performance and ethics, ensuring that you lead in a manner that is both compassionate and commanding.

Additionally, the concept of continuous improvement both for oneself and one's team is covered extensively; it is crucial as a leader to model the behaviors you wish to see in your team, and this chapter not only discusses the importance of personal development and lifelong learning but also gives practical strategies for fostering a culture of growth and innovation within your organization, ensuring that you and your team remain agile and informed in an ever-evolving world.

Each of these chapters is constructed with the intention to not only provide knowledge but to also instill a sense of purpose and action, ensuring that you, as a leader who believes in God, find not just the theory but also the practical, actionable steps needed to apply these lessons in real-world scenarios; through this book, you will gain not just insight but also tools that are immediately applicable, helping you to lead more effectively and ethically, aligned with your values and beliefs.

The main lesson from each chapter is meticulously detailed and paired with practical applications that you can start implementing right away, ensuring that the knowledge you gain from this book isn't just theoretical but truly transformational, enabling you to elevate your leadership and make a significant impact in your organization and community, all while staying true to your faith and the higher calling of service that leadership inherently involves.

By the end of this book, you will not only have a comprehensive skill set in leadership but also the confidence to apply these skills in a way that is respectful of your faith and supportive of your mission as a leader, making decisions that are not only effective but also righteous, and guiding your team towards success in a way that uplifts and inspires.

Know the Difference Between Who You Are and What You Do - Character

"God always uses flawed individuals who are willing to do His will. While it's commendable to accomplish great things as a leader, it's unhealthy to lose your identity. Who are you beyond your assignment? Do you seek balance in your professional and personal lives? Have you mistaken what for who? Find your security and identity in Christ, not your service or position."

Problems and Context

When the actions of a leader, who deeply believes in the guidance of a higher power, begin to define their very essence, a significant issue arises, one that complicates the foundational understanding of who they are versus what they do. Often, leaders find themselves in a whirlwind where their identity becomes indistinguishably tied to their professional roles, leading to a profound confusion that blurs the lines between personal identity and the responsibilities they hold. This entanglement can lead to decision-making processes that are not only flawed but are misaligned with their true character, as actions taken may more reflect the role expected of them rather than their genuine beliefs and values.

Imagine a scenario where a leader is prematurely judged based on the outcomes of their department or team—often a verdict that's reached before all evidence is laid out—and thus, they find themselves in the precarious position of having to justify actions that may not align with their personal integrity. Here, the leader is compelled to defend or rationalize decisions to align with the perceived notions of success and failure within their professional domain, rather than standing firm in their moral convictions. This situation puts enormous pressure on leaders, as they struggle to navigate the fine line between upholding their responsibilities and staying true to their core principles.

The impact of this confusion between personal identity and professional role becomes significantly consequential, not only on the leaders' decision-making processes but also on their integrity and moral compass. It's not uncommon to see decisions that are heavily influenced by the role's demands instead of being guided by ethical values and sincere judgment. This misalignment can lead to choices that might achieve short-term gains or appease certain expectations but ultimately detract from the leader's true character and personal beliefs.

This dilemma often escalates when leaders, acting out of a sense of role rather than conviction, find themselves justifying actions or policies that they might not inherently agree with. Such actions, although possibly effective in fulfilling role expectations, might chip away at their moral integrity and personal satisfaction. This constant tug-of-war can leave leaders feeling disconnected, discontent, and even dishonest with themselves, which can ripple out to affect their relationships with their teams, peers, and even their personal lives.

It becomes essential, then, for leaders who cherish their relationship with God and who aim to lead a life that's reflective of their faith, to discern clearly the line between their identity and their professional duties. Recognizing that what they do is a part of who they are—but not the entirety of their being—is crucial in maintaining not only their integrity but also their inner peace and satisfaction in their leadership roles. This understanding allows them to lead not just with efficiency but with authenticity and moral rectitude, ensuring that each decision, while it may fulfill a professional requirement, also resonates with their deeper, spiritual convictions.

When leaders navigate their roles with this clarity, they not only enhance their effectiveness but also model a way of leading that is deeply rooted in ethical values and personal integrity. This approach not only inspires trust and admiration from their followers but also fosters an environment where the same values are encouraged and replicated, creating a ripple effect that enhances the overall moral fabric of their organization. The importance of this cannot be overstated, especially in today's world where ethical leadership is both more challenging and more needed than ever.

In conclusion, the journey of distinguishing between 'who you are' and 'what you do' is not just about improving leadership effectiveness; it's about fostering a sense of genuine fulfillment and aligning one's professional life with one's deepest values and beliefs. For a leader who believes in God and strives to reflect God's will in their leadership, understanding and addressing the confusion between personal identity and professional role is not only beneficial but essential. It is the bedrock upon which they can build a legacy of leadership that is not only successful but also righteous and true to their calling.

Understanding Your Core Identity

As a leader who deeply values your faith and role in both your community and organization, it is quite essential to develop a clear understanding of the distinction between who you are at your core and the roles you fulfill in your professional life; this distinction is not just beneficial but fundamental to maintaining integrity and effectiveness in leadership. Recognizing and embracing your intrinsic values and beliefs form the bedrock of your identity, which remains constant irrespective of the positions you hold or the tasks before you, and this understanding serves as your compass, guiding your actions and decisions in a manner consistent with your deepest convictions. When leaders blur the lines between their personal identity and their professional roles, they often find themselves at risk of losing sight of their true selves, which can lead to decisions that are misaligned with their core beliefs, creating internal conflict and possibly diminishing their effectiveness as leaders.

In your journey as a leader who believes in God, it becomes imperative to employ techniques that help in clearly defining these personal values and beliefs, so that these elements can act as steadfast anchors in the stormy seas of professional challenges and ethical dilemmas. Engaging in regular reflection and self-assessment can be incredibly useful in this regard, allowing you to deepen your understanding of what truly matters most to you, what principles you refuse to compromise on, and how you view your purpose beyond the immediate demands of your role. This practice is not just about self-knowledge but also about setting a foundation for all future actions and decisions, ensuring they are always aligned with your true self, thereby avoiding the trap of becoming someone you are not just to meet external expectations or demands.

Moreover, the importance of separating who you are from what you do cannot be overstated, as this separation not only protects your identity from being consumed by your roles but also prevents the inherent values of your faith from being overshadowed by professional ambitions or pressures. It is not uncommon for leaders to become unintentional threats to their own core identities by allowing their roles to define their worth or success; however, by maintaining a clear boundary between your personal identity and your professional role, you safeguard your self-worth from being tied solely to your achievements or failures at work. This clarity enables you to perform your roles more effectively, as it allows you to engage fully without the fear of losing your identity in the process, and it also provides the freedom to innovate, take risks, and pursue excellence, knowing that your value as a person is not on the line.

Lastly, considering the challenges and pressures inherent in leadership, it is crucial to recognize when the storm is not just coming from external sources but is also being influenced by internal conflicts and pressures. This dual-edged nature of challenges can serve as both a moment for self-care and a revelation about your own resilience and the true nature of others around you. When you are clear about your core identity and have separated it from your professional roles, you can face these storms with a level of calm and assurance that comes from knowing who you are, which in turn allows you to manage stress and conflict more effectively. Engaging in regular self-care practices such as prayer, meditation, or simply spending time in reflection can be instrumental in maintaining this clarity and peace, enabling you to lead not just with effectiveness but with a sense of purpose and fulfillment that aligns with your deepest beliefs.

Understanding and maintaining your core identity as a leader who believes in God is not merely about personal satisfaction but about embodying the principles of your faith in every aspect of your leadership. This alignment not only enriches your life but also inspires those you lead, setting a powerful example of integrity and authenticity in leadership.

Role Clarity in Your Professional Life

In the realm of leadership and management, understanding the specific functions and responsibilities that define your professional role can be likened to a captain knowing the distinct parts and operations of a ship; this knowledge is paramount not just for the smooth sailing of the vessel, but also for the safety and efficiency of the entire crew aboard. When leaders clearly define their roles within the organizations they serve, they anchor themselves against the rough seas of confusion and inefficiency, enabling not only their personal growth but also enhancing the collective productivity of their teams. This clarity in role definition allows you to navigate through your professional environment with precision and to delegate tasks more effectively, ensuring that everyone on the team is right where they need to be, doing exactly what they are best at.

Moreover, the impact of role clarity extends beyond mere operational efficiency; it also significantly influences personal development and job satisfaction. When you, as a leader, understand the boundaries and expectations of your role, you are less likely to overextend yourself or step into areas that are outside your jurisdiction, which can often lead to stress and burnout. Imagine a scenario where your responsibilities are so intertwined with those of others that you find yourself constantly overlapping duties, doubling efforts, or even conflicting with colleagues. Such situations can be avoided when your

21

role is clearly delineated, respected, and understood not just by you but also by everyone you work with. This leads to a more harmonious workplace and allows for true professional growth where each individual's contributions are recognized and valued.

However, defining one's role isn't merely about setting boundaries; it's also about understanding when those boundaries need to be flexible. In the dynamic landscape of modern business, the ability to adapt and extend one's competencies without losing sight of core responsibilities is a valuable skill. When process is often replaced by preference, as seen in environments where 'how things are done' becomes less important than 'what is done', it is your role clarity that will prevent you from being swayed by every passing trend and help maintain a focus on outcomes that align with the organization's goals and values. Flexibility should not lead to a dilution of your foundational responsibilities but should enhance your ability to respond to changes effectively.

Furthermore, this flexibility should not lead to a scenario where preference defines everything, overshadowing established processes that ensure consistency and quality. Preference-driven environments risk creating a workspace where decisions are made based on personal biases rather than what is best for the team or project. Leaders must be vigilant and ensure that their flexibility in role does not compromise the integrity and effectiveness of their function within the organization. By maintaining a clear distinction between when to adhere to the process

22

and when to accommodate preferences, you safeguard the organization against erratic shifts and maintain a steady course towards its strategic objectives.

In summary, the clarity of your role within your professional sphere is not just about sticking to a list of tasks—it is about understanding the essence of your contributions, the impact of your leadership, and the dynamics of your interactions with others. This understanding is crucial not only for your own professional path but also for the broader health of the organization. It allows for a system where everyone knows their exact roles and how those roles contribute to the collective success. Leaders who master this balance between firm boundaries and adaptive flexibility are the ones who lead their teams to not just meet targets but to exceed them, fostering an environment of respect, efficiency, and progressive growth.

Aligning Personal and Professional Values

Every leader who believes in God understands the profound impact that personal values can have on their professional life, guiding decisions and interactions in a manner that reflects their deepest beliefs and principles; however, the journey to align these personal convictions with one's professional responsibilities is not always straightforward, requiring intentional strategies and a commitment to authenticity that transcends the superficial layer of daily tasks and enters the realm of moral leadership. To start, one must first recognize the intrinsic value of their personal beliefs, acknowledging that these are not just private matters but are essential foundations that should inform and guide leadership style and decisions, thus ensuring that actions taken in a professional capacity are not only effective but also ethically sound and aligned with one's deeper moral convictions. This alignment benefits leaders by fortifying their integrity and authenticity, making them not only more respected but also more fulfilled in their roles, for when leaders operate in congruence with their values, they exhibit a genuineness that is palpable and inspiring to those around them.

When considering the methods to ensure personal values guide your leadership style, it begins with a clear and honest assessment of what these values are—a task that might seem simple yet requires deep introspection and sincerity, for it involves distinguishing between what you genuinely believe and the values that are adopted superficially or imposed by external expectations. Once these values are clearly identified and embraced, the next step involves openly communicating these principles to your team and integrating them into the organizational culture, which might involve setting specific ethical guidelines, developing training programs that emphasize these values, or simply leading by example, where every decision and action reflects these guiding principles. This process not only helps in creating a cohesive team that shares a common set of values but also in building a strong organizational identity that can withstand external pressures and challenges.

However, aligning personal and professional values is not without its challenges, particularly when personal humility and professional ego collide, often leading to situations where leaders might downplay their achievements or strengths under the guise of humility, thereby inadvertently undermining their authority and effectiveness. In such cases, it is crucial to find a balance where humility does not transform into self-deprecation but rather fosters an environment where achievements are celebrated without arrogance, and failures are acknowledged without discouragement, all while maintaining a clear focus on the collective mission and the shared values that guide the organization. This balance is not only key to personal growth but also essential in cultivating a leadership style that is both assertive and compassionate, authoritative yet approachable, ultimately enhancing the leader's ability to guide effectively while remaining true to their core values.

Moreover, leaders often face situations where they feel they have more to contribute even after formal responsibilities have ended, a scenario that underscores the importance of viewing leadership not just as a role but as a lifelong commitment to ethical growth and service. In such instances, it is vital for leaders to seek other avenues to continue their service, be it through mentorship, community service, or continued personal development, thus ensuring that their journey of value-based leadership does not end with a particular assignment but evolves into a lasting legacy of influence and inspiration. This ongoing commitment to personal and professional development not only enriches the leader's life but also serves as a beacon to others, demonstrating that leadership is not confined to titles or roles but is a continuous pursuit of excellence and integrity.

In conclusion, aligning personal values with professional responsibilities is a dynamic and ongoing process that requires diligence, reflection, and an unwavering commitment to authenticity. It demands that leaders not only recognize and define their personal values but also actively strive to embody these principles in their professional lives, thereby fostering an environment of trust, respect, and genuine leadership. By embracing this alignment, leaders can ensure that their professional actions are not only effective but also profoundly impactful, reflecting a leadership style that is deeply rooted in ethical integrity and aimed at achieving not just organizational goals but also greater societal good.

Maintaining Boundaries Between Role and Identity

In the leadership path, one of the most fundamental aspects that every leader who believes in God should consider seriously is the establishment of clear boundaries between their professional role and personal identity; this separation is not merely about keeping work and personal life distinct, but it's an essential practice that fosters mental and spiritual well-being, preventing the common yet dangerous blend of personal self with professional obligations, which can often lead to a sense of loss in personal values and burnout. Achieving this requires a deliberate and conscious effort, where you, as a leader, recognize and implement practical steps that serve to demarcate your professional responsibilities from your personal beliefs and values, ensuring that while you serve in your role effectively, you do not allow this role to redefine who you are at your core.

To begin with, understanding the importance of boundaries in your leadership role involves appreciating that while your professional responsibilities demand certain behaviors and decisions, these do not necessarily have to align completely with your personal self; for example, you may be required to make tough decisions that affect other people's lives, which is a part of your job, yet, how you feel about these decisions should remain separate from your identity. This careful separation helps maintain your integrity and personal values intact, reducing the risk of internal conflicts and stress, which are often the results of a blurred line between personal ethics and professional duties. When leaders fail to maintain these boundaries, they risk their role consuming their personal identity, leading to burnout and a diminished sense of self-worth, which can be detrimental not only to their personal life but also to their effectiveness as leaders.

Therefore, it's crucial to take practical steps towards establishing these boundaries; one effective approach is to constantly self-reflect on your actions and decisions within your role, asking yourself whether

27

these are solely for the role's demands or if they are influenced by personal beliefs. By regularly analyzing your motivations and actions, you can gradually learn to distinguish between decisions made as a leader and those influenced by personal beliefs, which helps in maintaining a clear boundary. Additionally, setting specific work hours and sticking to them, delegating tasks appropriately, and taking regular breaks are all practical methods that help reinforce these boundaries, ensuring you do not carry the weight of your professional role into your personal life.

Another vital strategy to maintain this separation is to cultivate a strong support system both within and outside the workplace; discussing your thoughts and feelings about your role with trusted advisors or friends can provide you with insights and feedback that help you see when your role might be overshadowing your personal identity. Also, engaging in regular spiritual practices, such as prayer or meditation, can strengthen your inner peace and personal identity, giving you the clarity and strength needed to maintain boundaries between your role and your personal self. It is also beneficial to attend workshops or training on leadership and personal development, which can offer new techniques and perspectives on separating and balancing your professional and personal life.

In essence, the maintenance of clear boundaries between your professional role and personal identity is not just a matter of discipline but a profound commitment to your overall well-being and effectiveness as a leader. It requires a continuous effort, where you must be vigilant in protecting your personal values and beliefs while fulfilling your professional duties competently. By doing so, you not only enhance your leadership capabilities but also promote a sustainable career and life, where personal satisfaction and professional success are both attainable and maintained in harmony. As leaders, particularly those who look to their faith as a guiding principle, recognizing the importance of these boundaries and actively working to uphold them can be one of the most rewarding and liberating experiences, allowing you to lead with confidence and authenticity, grounded in the truth of who you are and inspired by the divine guidance you seek.

Recap and Actionable Steps

In this crucial section, we delve deeply into the often overlooked yet fundamentally significant distinction between your identity and your role, especially as a leader who holds faith close to their heart; understanding this difference is not just about improving how you lead, but also about enriching the way you live and interact with the world around you. Earlier chapters discussed the various impacts and the confusion that can stem from intertwining who you are with what you do—a mix-up that might seem minor on the surface but has profound implications on your integrity, decision-making, and overall personal growth.

As we move forward, it's essential to internalize that your core identity should guide your actions and decisions, irrespective of the professional hats you wear; this approach isn't just about maintaining personal harmony but is also pivotal in fostering genuine leadership that resonates with the values you cherish. When your actions as a leader are rooted deeply in your personal beliefs and values, not only do you stand as a beacon of authenticity and trust, but you also pave the way for others to explore and express their true selves, creating a ripple effect of authenticity and integrity throughout your organization or community.

Now, to aid you in this journey of aligning your personal values with your professional role without losing sight of either, here's a detailed, step-by-step guide designed to be immediately actionable and profoundly transformative:

Start by revisiting your core values and beliefs; write them down if you haven't already, and reflect on how these are represented in your daily actions and decisions.

Examine your current professional role and responsibilities; list them out and identify where there might be conflicts or misalignments with your personal values.

For each conflict identified, brainstorm potential solutions or adjustments you could make to better align your role with your values; this might involve delegating certain tasks, altering your approach to leadership, or even initiating conversations about change within your organization.

Implement the changes gradually but consistently, tracking progress and feelings of fulfillment or dissonance that arise as you align closer with your true self.

Regularly review this alignment; as you grow, both personally and professionally, your understanding of your values and how they translate into your role might evolve.

Maintain open communication with your peers, mentors, and team members about your values and leadership style; this not only helps in keeping you accountable but also encourages an environment where values and roles are openly discussed and respected.

By following these steps diligently, you will not only solidify the distinction between your identity and your professional role but also enhance your effectiveness and authenticity as a leader who believes in God. Your leadership will no longer just be about the decisions you make or the objectives you achieve but also about the values you embody and inspire in others, making your leadership journey not just a professional endeavor but a spiritual and personal one as well.

Remember, the journey to maintaining character in leadership roles is continuous and ever-evolving; it's about making consistent efforts to ensure your actions are always reflective of your deepest beliefs and values. Through this meticulous process, you forge not just a path of leadership but a legacy of character and faith that profoundly impacts all facets of your life and those around you.

Know the Difference Between Struggling and Transitioning - Decisiveness

"And Jacob awaked out of his sleep, and he said, Surely the LORD is in this place; and I knew it not. And he was afraid, and said, How dreadful is this place! this is none other but the house of God, and this is the gate of heaven." Genesis 28:16-17

Problems and Context

As a leader who holds faith dear, you understand that life's journey is punctuated by periods of difficulty and periods of change, both of which can appear similar at first glance but are fundamentally different in nature and how they should be approached; distinguishing between a natural transitional phase and true struggling is a critical skill that you need to develop to lead effectively and grow personally. This distinction is important because misinterpreting the challenges you face can lead to missteps in your leadership, causing unnecessary hardship for yourself and those you lead, and potentially stifling personal and professional growth instead of fostering it.

Imagine a scenario where a leader views every difficulty as a struggle, a battle to be fought with sheer grit; while perseverance is a valuable trait, understanding that some of these phases might actually be transitions calling for patience and strategic adjustments can dramatically change the outcome. Furthermore, when timing and priorities in leadership are not considered, decisions can become reactive rather than strategic, leading to choices that may not align with the long-term vision and goals of your organization or personal life, which often results in increased stress and decreased effectiveness.

Leaders are sometimes forced into positions where they must take sides due to external pressures or internal conflicts within their organization; this is particularly challenging when the decisions are more about survival—either of the leader's position or the organization's future—than about moving the organization forward in its mission. As a leader who believes in God, it's crucial to recognize that these moments of decision are not just about choosing sides but about understanding the broader context in which these decisions are made. This understanding can help you navigate through such times with wisdom and clarity, ensuring that your actions are aligned with your faith and your leadership values.

Therefore, recognizing whether you are in a phase of transition or if you are genuinely struggling is key to making informed, effective decisions. It involves an understanding of the nuances of each situation, an awareness of the long-term impacts of your decisions, and a willingness to adapt your leadership style to meet the needs of the moment without compromising your core values or the mission of your organization. By developing this skill, you enhance not only your capacity to lead with decisiveness but also your ability to guide your team through challenges with confidence and faith.

By working through these distinctions and becoming adept at identifying whether you are facing a transition or a struggle, you set the stage for more enlightened leadership—one that harmonizes with your beliefs and promotes a healthy, sustainable growth path for both you and your organization. This understanding also enables you to provide more effective support to your team, fostering an environment where challenges are met with strategic thinking and faith-driven resilience, rather than fear or confusion. So, let us delve deeper into understanding these concepts, ensuring that you are equipped to lead not just effectively, but profoundly, in alignment with your faith and the divine guidance you seek in your leadership role.

Recognizing Signs of Transition

When you, as a leader, find yourself faced with changes that might initially seem daunting or even insurmountable, it becomes imperative to distinguish whether these are mere struggles or signs of a significant transition; understanding this difference plays a crucial role in navigating through leadership challenges effectively and with God's guidance. Recognizing that you are in a phase of transition rather than struggle involves observing specific indicators that signal change, which is not merely about the struggles but about moving toward a God-ordained path that fosters growth and improvement in your role as a leader. Many leaders often mistake these times of change for periods of struggle, which can lead to unnecessary stress and misguided actions that may not align with God's plan.

To embrace and manage transitions in leadership, you must first understand the nature of transition itself; it is a process where old ways transform into new opportunities, and this transformation is guided by God's hand, leading you from one phase of your leadership journey to another. When you identify that you are in such a phase, it empowers you to take actions that align with this new direction rather than fighting against it, which is often the case when one perceives the situation as a struggle. Transition periods in leadership can often bring about feelings of uncertainty and discomfort; however, it is within these moments that God often works the most, refining your character and enhancing your ability to lead with wisdom and compassion.

Considering the season you are in is another vital aspect of managing transitions effectively; this involves acknowledging that there are times for growth, times for planting, times for reaping, and times for renewal, all within your leadership journey. Understanding that there is a divine timing for everything under heaven allows you to better align your actions with what is expected and required of you during each phase, thus facilitating smoother transitions and reducing the resistance that often comes with change. This acknowledgment helps in making informed decisions that are not rushed but are timely and reflective of the needs of the moment, which in turn, leads to more effective leadership and a greater impact on those you lead.

Finally, when there is division in the assignment, it becomes particularly important to recognize the signs of transition because such divisions often signify a need for a new direction or approach in leadership. Division can often be a clear indicator that the old ways are no longer working and that a new phase is on the horizon, urging you to shift strategies or perspectives to reunite and move forward. It's during these times that prayer and reflection become invaluable tools in discerning the right steps to take, ensuring that any changes in direction are in line with God's will and are aimed at bringing about unity and renewed purpose among your team members.

Understanding and addressing these elements not only aids in recognizing when you are transitioning but also equips you to handle these transitions with grace and effectiveness, ensuring that your leadership remains strong, resilient, and aligned with God's purpose for your life and the lives of those you lead. By embracing the transitions, you open up to new possibilities and opportunities for growth that God has prepared for you, making your leadership journey not just about guiding others but also about personal and spiritual growth that shapes you into the leader God intends you to be.

Strategies to Overcome Struggle

When it comes to overcoming the struggles that you, as a leader who believes in the guidance of a higher power, often encounter, it's vital to recognize that these challenges are not merely obstacles but are opportunities for growth and refinement of your leadership skills; it is imperative to develop techniques that not only address these struggles head-on but also allow you to emerge stronger and more resilient than before. The first step in this transformative process involves a deep and thoughtful introspection where you must identify the core of your struggles; this might mean recognizing where your expectations of outcomes deviate from the reality of your circumstances, which can be a revealing and sometimes challenging process.

One of the critical techniques to effectively manage and move beyond these struggles is to build resilience, not just in yourself but also within your team, which involves fostering an environment where challenges are viewed as catalysts for innovation rather than signs of impending failure. This perspective shift is crucial and requires consistent effort and reinforcement through positive affirmations and by setting examples through your actions, which demonstrate your faith in both your mission and the divine support guiding you. When you encounter painful situations, as a leader guided by strong faith, it's essential to put your pain in perspective; this doesn't mean dismissing your feelings but rather understanding them in the larger context of your role and responsibilities.

Another powerful strategy lies in recognizing that your struggles, while personally challenging, are not just about you; someone somewhere might be looking at how you handle these situations, and this could be inspiring them to handle their own challenges with grace and courage. This realization should empower you and serve as a motivation to handle your struggles with even greater diligence and faith, knowing that your actions are likely serving as a beacon of hope and strength to others. Thus, your approach to overcoming struggles should not only be about finding solutions for yourself but should also consider the broader impact of your journey on those around you, possibly turning your personal tests into testimonies that can uplift others.

By adopting these strategies, not only will you be able to address your current struggles more effectively, but you will also lay a robust foundation for proactive leadership. This proactive approach is about anticipating potential challenges and preparing for them before they escalate into more significant issues, which is a hallmark of a visionary leader. Moreover, embracing these strategies wholeheartedly and integrating them into your leadership style can transform the very nature of how you perceive and interact with challenges, ultimately leading to a more fulfilling and impactful leadership journey. Remember, every struggle is a step on the ladder of your leadership evolution, each with its lessons and blessings, designed to elevate you to higher levels of understanding and achievement in your divine calling.

Leveraging Transition for Growth

When a leader who believes in God finds themselves in a period of transition, it is an incredible opportunity that should not be seen lightly, as these times are rich with the potential for significant personal and professional development that aligns with their spiritual beliefs and leadership responsibilities; understanding this concept deeply and embracing the opportunities it presents can lead to a fulfilling and impactful progression in both their life and the lives of those they lead. It is important to recognize that transitions, though sometimes uncomfortable and filled with uncertainty, are not just random occurrences but are often divine setups for greater growth and success, which is why it's crucial to approach them with a mindset that seeks out growth and learning. Transition periods are times when God might be preparing you for a new chapter, and thus, they require a thoughtful assessment of where you are and where you need to go, both as a person and a leader.

Your call in life, which is often much bigger than the specific assignments you handle day-to-day, finds a unique expression during these times of transition; it is in these moments that you can truly reflect on the broader impact of your work and how it aligns with your higher calling, making it essential to not only continue to meet daily responsibilities but also to keep an eye on the larger picture. Prioritizing issues becomes an act of wisdom and discernment, as it involves understanding which challenges should be addressed immediately and which ones should be planned for more strategically, ensuring that both immediate needs and long-term goals are met in a balanced manner. This practice of prioritizing not only helps in managing the transition effectively but also in setting a solid foundation for future successes, providing a clear path forward in times that might otherwise feel overwhelming or directionless.

By actively seeking to understand the nature of the transitions you are experiencing, you can begin to outline steps for leveraging these periods for your growth, which involves identifying the skills, attitudes, and resources that will be most beneficial in navigating this phase successfully. One actionable way to leverage transitions is to enhance your networking efforts, reaching out to mentors and peers who have navigated similar changes, as their insights and support can prove invaluable in providing guidance and encouragement. Furthermore, setting specific, measurable, achievable, relevant, and time-bound (SMART) goals during transitions can help in maintaining focus and momentum, ensuring that you are making measurable progress even when the path forward might seem unclear or cluttered with obstacles.

Another critical aspect is maintaining a strong spiritual foundation, as your faith can provide the strength and wisdom needed during uncertain times; daily practices such as prayer, meditation, and scripture reading can help in staying connected to your beliefs and values, which are essential for inner peace and clarity when external circumstances are in flux. Moreover, embracing a mindset of gratitude during transitions can significantly alter your perspective, helping you to see each challenge as an opportunity to learn and each setback as a setup for a comeback, thereby maintaining a positive outlook that attracts further positivity and opportunities into your life.

In conclusion, transitions are not to be feared but embraced as they are rich with opportunities for growth and development, both personally and professionally; by understanding the nature of the transition, prioritizing effectively, setting SMART goals, maintaining a strong spiritual foundation, and adopting a mindset of gratitude, you can navigate these periods with grace and effectiveness, turning potential challenges into powerful pathways to success. Leaders who approach transitions with such a perspective are not only able to enhance their own lives but are also better equipped to lead others through change, demonstrating the strength, resilience, and wisdom that true leadership entails. Therefore, as you face transitions, remember that they are divine opportunities for enhancement and embrace them wholeheartedly, knowing that they are key to your growth and your ability to make a meaningful impact as a leader who believes in God.

Preventing Unnecessary Struggle

When we talk about leading without facing unnecessary hardships, it begins with understanding that struggles, while a natural part of life and leadership, can be minimized with proactive steps; this is critical because as leaders who hold faith dear, you recognize that every challenge presents both a test and a testimony, hence, preventing undue struggle not only eases your leadership journey but also strengthens your spiritual and professional resolve.

Firstly, one of the foundational steps to avoid common pitfalls that lead to struggle involves fostering a supportive environment; this approach is not merely about creating a physical space that is conducive to work, but more significantly, about cultivating an atmosphere where openness, trust, and mutual respect are paramount, because when your team members feel valued and understood, the likelihood of conflicts that can escalate into struggles decreases substantially.

Moreover, embracing the blessing called frustration might seem counterintuitive, yet it is a potent strategy in your leadership toolkit; often, frustration arises from situations where expectations do not meet reality, however, by redefining frustration as an opportunity to reassess and realign your goals, you not only prevent the escalation of these feelings into larger struggles but also empower your team to view challenges through a lens of growth and possibility, thereby maintaining a clear focus on collective goals rather than individual setbacks.

Techniques for maintaining decisiveness during challenging transitions also play a crucial role in preventing unnecessary struggles; it's about making informed decisions swiftly and confidently, which involves being thoroughly prepared with all the necessary information, consulting with trusted advisers, and most importantly, praying for wisdom and guidance, as these steps ensure that you are not paralyzed by indecision—which often complicates situations and transforms manageable issues into significant struggles.

Understanding these strategies and integrating them into your leadership approach is not just about avoiding difficulties but about setting a course that aligns with your divine purpose and enables you to lead with both conviction and compassion, championing not just the causes you believe in but also the people who look up to you for direction and inspiration.

Remember, every step you take to minimize struggle is a step towards a more effective, empathetic, and empowering leadership journey, so use these strategies wisely to not only enhance your capabilities but also to serve as a beacon of hope and resilience for those you lead.

Recap and Actionable Steps

Throughout this chapter, we explored the intricate differences between struggling and transitioning, two concepts that often appear similar at first glance but are fundamentally distinct in their impact on leadership and personal growth. Struggles often feel like roadblocks, complete with frustration and a sense of being stuck without forward movement; on the other hand, transitions are like the motion of stepping from one stone to another across a stream, where the challenge lies not in the step itself but in maintaining balance and focus on the destination ahead. It's imperative for a leader to recognize these differences because understanding them profoundly influences how one leads and grows amidst challenges and changes.

Now, let's distill what we've learned into concrete steps that you, as a leader who believes in greater guidance, can take to transform the knowledge into action. The goal is not only to manage these phases effectively but also to harness them as powerful catalysts for personal and professional growth. Here are some actionable steps designed to help you navigate transitions and overcome struggles with decisiveness and faith-driven strength:

Identify the Phase: Begin by categorizing the current challenge you are facing: is it a struggle or a transition? Remember, struggles are characterized by feelings of being stuck, while transitions involve movement towards change. Write down the symptoms and signs you observe, and pray for discernment to understand the nature of your situation.

Seek Guidance and Wisdom: Once you've identified the phase, seek divine guidance through prayer and reflection. Consult with trusted mentors who share your faith and values. Their insights can often shine a light on aspects you might not have considered and offer spiritual and practical advice tailored to your circumstances.

Establish Clear Objectives: In both struggles and transitions, clear objectives act as your north star. Define what success looks like in this phase. Is it overcoming a particular challenge, or successfully managing change? Set SMART goals (Specific, Measurable, Achievable, Relevant, Time-bound) that align with your ultimate purpose as a leader.

Develop a Strategic Plan: With your objectives in mind, develop a plan that includes specific actions, timelines, and resources needed. This plan should reflect both the immediate steps to manage current issues and longer-term strategies for ensuring continuous growth and stability.

Implement with Faith and Flexibility: As you implement your plan, remain flexible to adjustments along the way. Transition phases, in particular, can be unpredictable, and new insights can emerge that might require you to shift your approach. Maintain a strong faith, knowing that you are guided and supported in your journey.

Reflect and Adjust Regularly: Regular reflection is crucial. Schedule weekly or monthly review sessions to assess your progress against the goals you've set. This is not just about tracking success or setbacks but also about understanding the deeper lessons these experiences are teaching you. Make adjustments as necessary, always aligned with your core values and leadership vision.

Share Your Learnings: As a leader, your journey can inspire others. Share your experiences of managing struggles and transitions with your team, your community, or even in your personal blog or talks. Your stories can empower others to see their challenges in a new light and find their own paths through faith and leadership.

By following these steps, you will not only navigate struggles and transitions more effectively but also strengthen your leadership and deepen your connection with divine guidance. Each challenge you face is an opportunity to grow closer to your purpose and to demonstrate the power of faith in action. Remember, leadership is not just about personal success but about inspiring and uplifting those you lead, guiding them through their own struggles and transitions. Let your light shine as an example of what faithful, decisive leadership can achieve in the face of any challenge.

Know the Difference Between Projections and Reality - Worldview

"For as he thinketh in his heart, so is he..."

Proverbs 23:7

Problems and Context

As leaders who hold strong beliefs in divine power and guiding principles, it is essential to grasp the nuanced difference between how situations are perceived and the stark reality of those situations, a task that is not only challenging but could significantly alter the course of our decisions and hence, our leadership effectiveness. This understanding plays a pivotal role, as often, we may find ourselves inclined to base significant decisions on perceptions which, although seemingly concrete, might only be reflections of our desires or fears rather than the actual state of affairs. By recognizing this distinction, leaders can avoid the trap of making decisions that are misaligned with reality, decisions that could lead to consequences that impact not only themselves but their teams and organizations as a whole.

The implications of not distinguishing between perception and reality can be profound, impacting leadership decisions in ways that might not be immediately apparent but are nonetheless detrimental. For instance, when leaders interpret enthusiastic opinions as concrete evidence of a strategy's success, they might be overlooking underlying issues that could later surface and undermine their efforts. This reliance on opinion over factual evidence can lead to misguided strategies that do not address the core issues at hand. Moreover, when leaders operate under misperceptions, they risk not only the integrity of their decisions but also the trust and the morale of their teams, who look up to them for guidance and clarity.

Furthermore, a common occurrence in many organizations is when the enthusiasm of builders, those charged with creating and maintaining systems, is dampened by the criticisms of the so-called destruction crew, or those who focus solely on problems without contributing to solutions. This dynamic can lead to a toxic work environment where negativity prevails, stifling creativity and progress. Leaders must be adept at navigating these challenges, recognizing the difference between constructive criticism and destructive negativity, and ensuring that their perceptions are not clouded by the louder, perhaps more negative voices.

In conclusion, the ability to differentiate between perception and reality is crucial for effective leadership. This skill helps prevent the derailment of projects and initiatives due to misaligned strategies based on incorrect perceptions. It also plays a critical role in maintaining a positive and productive organizational culture, where facts and constructive feedback drive progress rather than opinions and negativity. By fostering an environment where reality is clearly distinguished from perception, leaders can ensure that their decisions are based on solid ground, leading to better outcomes for themselves and their teams.

Understanding the Impact of Perceptions

When leaders gather their teams together and discuss future strategies, having a clear and accurate understanding of the various perceptions that each member holds can be transformative; imagine the scenario where you, as a leader, believe in one direction while your team sees another path as being more feasible, and this disparity in views can lead to confusion or misaligned efforts, which is why it's crucial to understand and manage these perceptions actively. To begin with, techniques to assess and correct misperceptions in the workplace are not just about finding out what people think, but rather why they think that way, and how these thoughts influence their actions and decisions within the organizational framework, thereby, employing methods such as surveys, feedback sessions, and one-on-one conversations can provide a wealth of insight into what your team believes and perceives about the current workplace environment.

Furthermore, it is not only about collecting data, but also about interpreting it correctly and taking appropriate action based on this information, which is where the importance of gathering diverse perspectives comes into play; this approach helps to broaden the understanding and reduces the risk of echo chambers that can sometimes plague decision-making processes within leadership. By incorporating viewpoints from all levels of the organization, and possibly even from external stakeholders, leaders can form a more comprehensive picture of the reality, move towards it strategically, and thus make more informed and effective decisions that align well with the actual needs and conditions of the organization.

In addition to gathering diverse perspectives, it becomes pertinent when those you serve within your organization or community begin to voice their truths, which might be a reflection of their perceptions or their experienced realities; listening actively to these expressions can shed light on areas where there might be misalignments or misunderstandings between leadership projections and the ground realities. By acknowledging and validating these voices, leaders can foster a culture of trust and openness, encouraging more individuals to come forward, which in turn enhances the quality and accuracy of the collected insights.

Lastly, managing conflicting perceptions within teams is another vital area that requires thoughtful strategies and a proactive approach; it involves recognizing the existence of differing views, understanding the root causes of these differences, and then facilitating discussions or workshops to address and reconcile these discrepancies. This process not only helps in reducing conflicts but also aids in building a stronger, more cohesive team that is capable of collaborative problem-solving and innovation. By implementing such strategies, you ensure that your leadership is not only informed by a multifaceted view of organizational realities but is also resilient in the face of challenges posed by diverse perceptions and interpretations.

Through the detailed exploration of these techniques and strategies, every leader who believes in a higher purpose can better align their team's perceptions with the organizational realities, thereby enhancing decision-making processes, strengthening team cohesion, and leading with a vision that is not only aspirational but also grounded in the practical and varied experiences of those they lead. This thoughtful approach to understanding and managing perceptions is not just about correcting misalignments but is fundamentally about creating an environment where truth and transparency are the cornerstones of collective progress and success.

Tools to Uncover Reality

As leaders who hold their faith close, it is essential to recognize the role that discernment and truth play in guiding decisions and shaping the environments we are responsible for; methods to cut through bias and uncover the true nature of challenges within leadership are not merely tools, they are necessities that allow us to align our actions with the values we uphold. To begin with, the use of data and feedback in leadership can be significantly effective, not because they offer a magical solution to all problems, but because they provide tangible evidence that can help differentiate between what is perceived and what is real, ensuring that our decisions are grounded in facts rather than assumptions. When leaders harness the power of accurate data, coupled with honest feedback from teams and stakeholders, it becomes possible to paint a clearer picture of the current situations and challenges faced by organizations.

An important aspect of utilizing data effectively is understanding its source and context—data should not be taken at face value without considering where it comes from and what it represents, as doing so might lead to decisions based on skewed or incomplete information. This cautious approach is crucial because, as leaders, recognizing the origin and the context of the data helps us avoid misinterpretations that could lead to decisions that might not only be flawed but could also mislead others who depend on our judgment. Furthermore, when others choose to use their voice and influence to support your leadership—through mechanisms like petitions—it becomes even more important to ensure that the reality you are acting upon is not just your perception but a collective agreement on what is true and what needs attention, fostering an environment where transparency isn't just a word, but a practice that is lived out daily.

Techniques for fostering an environment of truth and transparency involve more than just an open-door policy or regular meetings; they require a consistent commitment to being open to challenges and criticisms, and a willingness to adapt and change based on what these truths reveal. This might seem daunting because it involves vulnerability, a trait that many may not associate with strong leadership, yet it is this very vulnerability that builds trust and loyalty, qualities that are indispensable in any leader's toolbox. A transparent leader does not shy away from hard truths but embraces them as a means to not only improve themselves but also to empower those they lead, making it clear that the path to improvement and growth is a shared journey, not a solitary endeavor.

In conclusion, the tools to uncover reality in leadership are not just about implementing systems or practices but about cultivating an attitude and a culture where truth prevails over convenience or ease It is about making tough choices, sometimes going against the grain and facing unpleasant facts, but always with the aim of upholding the values that define us as leaders who believe in a higher purpose and striving to serve in ways that are not only effective but also honorable and just. By committing to these practices, leaders can ensure that their actions and decisions not only lead to success in terms of outcomes but also in terms of integrity and ethical leadership, which are ultimately the hallmarks of true leadership.

Aligning Perception with Reality

When leaders who believe in a higher power look at their teams and organizations, they often see things through a lens shaped by their values and beliefs, which is a good thing, but sometimes, this lens can distort the way things really are, making it hard to align perceptions with actual circumstances, and that's when knowing how to realign these perceptions becomes essential. It's like having a map that doesn't match the terrain; no matter how much faith you have in your map, it won't be helpful if it doesn't reflect the landscape you're navigating through, and in an organizational context, this can lead to decisions that are not only ineffective but potentially harmful to the long-term health and growth of your organization.

One effective strategy to bring team and organizational perceptions in line with reality involves the implementation of regular training sessions that are designed not only to educate but also to open the floor for dialogue among team members. In these training sessions, leaders should focus on presenting factual, data-driven insights about the organization's performance, market trends, and other relevant metrics, giving every team member the same foundational understanding of where the organization stands, which is crucial because when everyone starts from the same set of facts, the discourse that follows is more likely to lead to conclusions rooted in reality rather than misperception.

Additionally, communication tactics play a pivotal role in reducing perceptual gaps within an organization, as regular, clear, and open communication ensures that all team members are on the same page, reducing the chances of misinformation spreading and taking root. A good practice is to hold weekly review meetings where team members can report on their progress, discuss challenges, and provide updates on their projects; this creates a culture of transparency and continuous feedback, which helps in keeping everyone's perceptions closely aligned with the actual state of affairs.

Moreover, methods for addressing and correcting false narratives within the organization are equally important, because sometimes, despite the best efforts, false stories can spread within teams, often fueled by misunderstandings or incorrect assumptions. Leaders need to be vigilant and proactive in addressing these narratives; this can be done by first identifying the root cause of the misinformation, whether it's a lack of information, miscommunication, or perhaps bias, and then addressing it directly and publicly, clarifying the facts and reaffirming the organization's values and objectives, which reassures team members and helps in realigning their perceptions with reality.

Finally, approaches to build a shared understanding of organizational realities involve not just correcting errors but actively building an environment where truth is actively sought and valued above convenience or expedience. This might involve setting up a dedicated internal communications channel where achievements, as well as failures, are discussed openly, or perhaps establishing a 'reality check' team tasked with periodically assessing projects and initiatives to ensure they are being pursued on the basis of accurate, up-to-date information, which helps in creating a culture where truth and transparency are not just encouraged but are part of the organization's very fabric.

For every leader who believes in guiding their team not just with spiritual wisdom but also with a grounded sense of reality, understanding these strategies and implementing them within your organization will not only help in making better, more informed decisions but will also foster a culture of trust and transparency where every team member feels valued and understood, creating a harmonious environment that is conducive to both personal and professional growth.

Managing Misperceptions

In the realm of leadership, especially for those who hold their faith and values close, the challenge of managing misperceptions can often seem like a daunting task; however, understanding how to adeptly navigate through these scenarios is critical in maintaining not only personal integrity but also the harmony and effectiveness of your team. When perceptions that are not based in reality begin to influence decisions and relationships, it is your role as a leader to step forward with both transparency and accountability, to guide your team back to a grounded understanding of the situation. This approach is not about correcting others just for the sake of asserting what's right but about nurturing an environment where truth and understanding flourish.

One of the primary techniques in managing misperceptions involves the upfront and consistent use of transparent communication. When you, as a leader, make it a standard practice to share your thoughts, intentions, and the rationale behind decisions, you create a culture of openness that discourages misinterpretations from taking root. It is crucial here to communicate not just the 'what' of your decisions but the 'why' as well; this deeper level of engagement with your team helps to preclude misunderstandings by providing them with a clear framework within which they can view your actions and decisions.

Accountability plays a twin role with transparency in the management of perceptions. By holding yourself accountable to your team, you set an example that accountability is valued and expected in your organization. This can be done by openly acknowledging any missteps or errors in judgment you make, thereby demonstrating that it is normal and acceptable to admit faults and work towards correcting them. This behavior promotes a culture where team members feel safe to express concerns or contradictions they perceive without fear of retribution or dismissal, which is essential in correcting misperceptions effectively.

When it comes to the diplomatic correction of misperceptions, your approach should be characterized by empathy and respect. Understanding that perceptions are often closely tied to personal values and emotions is key in addressing them gently and effectively. As a leader, approach these conversations with the intent to understand and bridge gaps in perception, not just to advocate for your own viewpoint. This involves actively listening to the concerns of team members, validating their feelings, and gradually guiding them towards a fuller understanding of the reality of the situation. These conversations, while potentially challenging, are vital in realigning team perceptions with organizational goals and realities.

Lastly, maintaining credibility in the face of false projections involves a consistent commitment to your values and the truth. This commitment needs to be visible in your actions, decisions, and the way you communicate. When false projections do arise, addressing them swiftly and factually can help in mitigating their impact. It is beneficial to have established a prior pattern of honest and transparent communication as this provides a solid foundation of trust from which you can more effectively counteract any false narratives.

Remember, the goal in managing misperceptions is not merely to assert what is right but to foster an environment where truth can be discussed openly and constructively. By fostering a culture of transparency, accountability, empathy, and respect, you safeguard your team not only against misperceptions but also against the potential divisiveness they can cause. Through these concerted efforts, you uphold not just the operational integrity of your team but also its moral spirit, aligning both with the deeper values that you, as a leader who believes in God, hold dear.

Recap and Actionable Steps

As leaders who hold faith close, understanding the distinction between perceptions and reality is paramount, not just for the integrity of our leadership but also for the nourishing of our souls and those we lead;

this clarity is what allows us to serve not just with our minds but with our hearts aligned with divine guidance. The journey through the various methods and strategies outlined in previous sections has equipped us with the tools necessary to pierce through the veils of bias and misperception, enabling us to lead our teams with a vision that closely mirrors the truth of our circumstances. To encapsulate the essence of what we've learned and to ensure that these insights translate into daily practice, here is a detailed recap along with actionable steps that you can implement immediately to maintain an accurate worldview in your leadership role.

Firstly, we must consistently remind ourselves that our perception of a situation may not necessarily reflect its reality; this understanding is crucial and forms the bedrock of effective leadership. Leaders who believe in God know that truth and integrity are non-negotiable, but even the best of us can falter if we do not actively seek out the reality of our environment. Thus, it is advisable to begin each day, or any major decision-making process, with a prayer or a moment of reflection, asking for the clarity to see things as they truly are, beyond our personal biases or fears.

Conduct Regular Reality Checks: Allocate time each week to review decisions and perceptions with your team. Use these meetings not just to assess the outcomes of decisions but to openly discuss the thoughts and perceptions that led to these decisions. This practice encourages transparency and continuous learning.

Implement a 'Perception Audit' System: Create a system where team members can anonymously submit their perceptions about significant projects or decisions. This can be as simple as a shared document or a more formal software tool. Regularly review these inputs and discuss them with your team to identify any common misperceptions or gaps between perception and reality.

Utilize Feedback for Alignment: Encourage and establish a culture where feedback is not only accepted but actively sought. Feedback sessions should be structured to provide insights into how team members perceive various aspects of the workplace and leadership decisions. This regular feedback mechanism acts as a compass, guiding leadership to align more closely with the team's perceived and actual needs.

Engage in Community and Spiritual Reflection: As leaders in faith, engage with your community and spiritual texts to reflect on the morals and teachings that emphasize truth and reality. Such engagement provides a moral compass, continually guiding against the drift towards misperceptions.

Develop a Personal Checklist for Decision Making: Craft a checklist that includes questions designed to challenge your current perceptions. Questions could include: "What are the facts supporting this view?", "Have I sought out diverse opinions?", and "Am I allowing my emotions to cloud my judgement?". This checklist should be used diligently before making strategic decisions.

Finally, it is essential to create a habit loop around these practices to ensure they become ingrained in your leadership style. Each step should be revisited regularly to foster an environment where reality and perception are not just occasionally aligned, but are consistently in sync, allowing for leadership that is not only effective but profoundly impactful and aligned with our deepest beliefs. By maintaining a clear and truthful perspective, you harness not only the power of effective leadership but also fulfill a spiritual mandate that elevates both your role and the lives of those you lead towards greater fulfillment and success.

Know the Difference Between What You Know and How You Feel - Attitude

"Finally, brethren, whatsoever things are true, whatsoever things are honest, whatsoever things are just, whatsoever things are pure, whatsoever things are lovely, whatsoever things are of good report; if there be any virtue, and if there be any praise, think on these things."
Phillipians 4:8

Problems and Context

In the journey of leadership, particularly for those who lead guided by faith, one significant hurdle often encountered is the intrinsic conflict between emotional responses and the necessity for informed decision-making, a challenge that persists regardless of the leader's experience or sphere of influence. When leaders, who are often looked up to as beacons of guidance and decision, allow their unchecked emotions to dominate, the result can often lead to decisions that might not align well with the principles or the mission they stand for; this is particularly critical for you, as a leader who believes in grounding actions in faith and principle. It is crucial to recognize that while emotions are integral

62

to our human experience, they must be managed with care to ensure they do not undermine the effectiveness of your leadership.

Imagine a situation where you, as a leader, face a high-stress situation that could easily provoke a strong emotional response; in such moments, it's essential to remember that your guiding absolutes, the core principles derived from your faith and ethical standpoint, remain intact and should guide your actions. The ability of a leader to stand firmly by these guiding absolutes, even when emotions run high, is what often separates effective leaders from the rest. It is when these principles define not only your personal practices but extend into policies and preferences within your organization, that a robust leadership foundation is built — one that is less likely to be shaken by the storms of emotional turmoil.

The key here lies in the conscious effort to ensure that these principles are not just posters on the wall but are lived out in the daily operational and strategic decisions made. This alignment is crucial, for it not only strengthens your leadership but also sets a clear example for others within your organization, emphasizing the importance of principle over impulse. Such a practice not only fosters a stronger organizational culture but also contributes to a more consistent and predictable leadership approach, elements that are incredibly valued in any leadership role, especially within contexts that are dynamic and fraught with rapid changes.

In summary, as a leader who believes in the power and guidance of a higher being, the challenge lies not in the awareness of these emotions but in the effective management and alignment of them with the unchanging principles that define your leadership ethos. This alignment is crucial not just for personal leadership effectiveness but also sets the tone for how the organization navigates its own challenges. By consistently choosing principle over impulse, you not only uphold the integrity of your leadership but also model a pathway for others to follow, a pathway marked by stability, ethical integrity, and decision-making that transcends the fluctuations of emotional responses. Therefore, it's imperative to regularly reflect on your decisions and actions, ensuring they align with the core principles you advocate and hold dear; this practice not only enhances personal leadership but fundamentally strengthens the organization's cultural fabric, making it resilient against the inevitable emotional and ethical challenges that arise in any leadership journey.

Recognizing Emotional Triggers

When we think about being a leader who believes in God, there's an inherent understanding that our actions, reactions, and beliefs are guided not just by our own will, but by the divine wisdom that shapes our moral and ethical views; understanding our emotional triggers forms a crucial part of this journey, allowing us to respond to situations not with immediate emotion, but with measured, thoughtful reflection that aligns with our deeper values. Identifying both personal and professional triggers is the first step in this introspective process, as it helps us recognize those specific situations or behaviors in others that elicit strong emotional reactions from us, which can range from irritation to anger, or from anxiety to sadness, all of which can cloud our judgment and lead us away from making decisions that reflect our true beliefs and divine guidance. This identification process is deeply personal and requires an honest self-assessment where you ask yourself about those times when your emotions got the better of you, not to criticize yourself, but to understand better.

Techniques for emotional self-regulation, especially in high-stakes environments, become indispensable tools in the arsenal of a God-believing leader because these techniques allow us to maintain our composure, uphold our duties, and make decisions that are not just fair but divinely inspired. Emotional self-regulation involves a series of steps that start with recognizing the physiological signs of emotional arousal—like an increased heartbeat, faster breathing, or feeling heat flush through your body—followed by a conscious decision to not let these initial reactions dictate your actions. The practice might include taking deep breaths, a moment of prayer or meditation, or simply choosing to respond with forgiveness rather than bitterness and resentment, which not only aligns with Christian teachings but also diffuses potentially volatile situations and turns them into opportunities for reconciliation and understanding, thus fostering an environment where dialogue and peace prevail over conflict and discord.

Strategies for maintaining composure in emotionally charged situations are crucial, as these are the moments when leadership is truly tested, and the eyes of both subordinates and superiors are on you to guide them through the storm; maintaining composure isn't about suppressing your emotions but understanding them, channeling them constructively, and responding in a way that is testament to your faith and your role as a leader. This might involve pausing before reacting, which not only gives you time to process your emotions but also to seek guidance through prayer and reflection, ensuring that your response is measured and in line with your spiritual and leadership values. Such strategies not only strengthen your leadership but also set a powerful example for others on how to handle their emotions, particularly in settings where the easy response would be to react out of fear, anger, or frustration.

Every leader who believes in God knows that their journey is not just about guiding others but about continually evolving and refining their own character according to divine will, and understanding the dynamics of emotional triggers and how to manage them effectively is a vital part of this process. It's about turning each emotionally charged situation into a testament of your faith, where your initial response is forgiveness, not bitterness and resentment, reflecting not only on your personal growth but also enhancing your effectiveness as a leader who is looked upon as a representative of both their faith and their people. Hence, the management of emotional triggers is not just about personal peace but about embodying the principles of leadership and faith that you stand for, making your leadership not just effective but truly inspired.

Leveraging Emotional Intelligence

When we talk about leveraging emotional intelligence to enhance leadership effectiveness, we're essentially discussing the intricate dance of understanding not just your own emotions, but also those of the people around you, which leads to better teamwork, smoother conflict resolution, and ultimately, more effective leadership. Emotional intelligence is your ability to recognize and understand emotions in yourself and others, and your ability to use this awareness to manage your behavior and relationships, which, for a leader, is as critical as any technical skill. What makes emotional intelligence truly special for leaders is its capacity to transform not just individual interactions but also to sculpt the emotional landscape of an entire organization.

Now, the importance of empathy in understanding team dynamics cannot be overstated because empathy allows you to see the world from another person's perspective and to share in their emotional experience, which is invaluable in leadership. By fostering empathy, you as a leader can create an environment of open communication and trust, which is fundamental for successful team dynamics; it's about more than just being nice—it's about genuinely understanding your team's thoughts, feelings, and perspectives, which in turn helps in crafting strategies that make everyone feel valued and understood. When you understand what motivates your team and what concerns them, you can address issues before they become problems, tailor your communication to meet their needs, and build a stronger, more cohesive unit.

There are moments in leadership when silence can indeed be your only true voice, when choosing not to react immediately or to offer an opinion provides others the space to express themselves and can lead to deeper understanding and resolution of complex issues; this kind of silence isn't about inactivity but is a strategic tool for enhancing dialogue and reflection. By embracing silence, you give others the room to fill the void with their thoughts and feelings, which can often lead to insights that words can sometimes obscure. Silence, used wisely, is a powerful component of emotional intelligence that allows a leader to gather information, absorb it, and then use it to guide decision-making.

Finally, developing techniques for reading and responding to others' emotional states is a skill that can significantly enhance your leadership. This means not just noticing the obvious signs of distress or happiness but also picking up on the subtler cues like body language, tone of voice, and facial expressions, which can tell you a lot about what someone is feeling but not saying. This skill allows you to respond more effectively because you're addressing not just the surface issues but also the underlying emotions that could be influencing someone's behavior.

For instance, if a team member is showing signs of stress, a leader skilled in emotional intelligence can recognize those signs early and offer support or adjust workloads before the stress leads to burnout or conflict.

By focusing on these aspects of emotional intelligence, leaders can enhance their effectiveness and create a workplace environment that is not only productive but also supportive and responsive to the emotional needs of their team members. This not only improves the morale and well-being of the team but also drives performance and success, making emotional intelligence not just a personal skill but a professional strategy that can differentiate a good leader from a great one.

Balancing Emotions with Factual Knowledge

When you, as a leader who believes in God, step forward to make a decision that could potentially affect many people, not only within your organization but perhaps even beyond it, there lies a profound responsibility on your shoulders to weigh not just what your heart feels but also what the facts state; this balancing act is not just about being efficient in your role, but it's about embodying the wisdom that comes from a place of deep reflection and understanding, where every choice is not just a reflection of your personal emotions or inclinations but is deeply rooted in the factual reality that surrounds the circumstances you are dealing with.

Now, to ensure that your decisions are as balanced as possible, it is essential to have tools that can help you separate emotional inputs from factual data, and this begins by recognizing that both elements play critical roles in leadership; your emotions can provide you with insights about the values, concerns, and motivations of both yourself and others, which are invaluable, yet the factual data provides a grounding point, a reality check that helps ensure that the decisions made are not only empathetic but also practical and sustainable in the long term.

One effective method for integrating emotional insights with factual analysis is to maintain a decision journal, which helps in recording not only the decisions made but also the emotional state and the factual basis for these decisions; this practice can help you observe patterns over time, providing insights into how your emotions influence your decisions and how outcomes are tied to these influences, thereby offering a structured way to reflect and learn from past experiences, ensuring that you grow not only as a leader but also as a person who seeks wisdom from every experience.

Furthermore, it is crucial to cultivate a habit of seeking counsel from diverse perspectives, which can involve having a trusted group of advisors who can offer both emotional and factual feedback on your ideas and plans; this group should ideally consist of individuals who not only understand your vision and share your values but also have the courage to challenge your ideas and add perspectives that might not align with your initial thoughts, thus providing a more rounded view that will enrich your decision-making process.

Moreover, investing time in regular training and development sessions focused on emotional intelligence can significantly enhance your ability to discern between when emotions are guiding you in a positive direction and when they might be clouding your judgment, thereby improving your capability to integrate these emotional insights with factual data effectively; such training often involves scenarios and role-play exercises that simulate challenging decision-making situations, allowing you to practice and hone your skills in a safe and supportive environment.

In conclusion, as a leader who believes in God, you are called upon not just to lead with authority but with wisdom that comes from a balanced approach to every decision, where both heart and head are aligned in such a way that your choices not only reflect your values and the emotional depth of your understanding but also the undeniable reality of the situation, grounded in facts and practicality; this balance is not just beneficial, it is essential for leadership that is not only effective but also righteous and true to the principles you stand for.

Training for Emotional Resilience

Leaders who hold firm beliefs in their faith often encounter scenarios where their emotional strength is tested just as much as their leadership abilities; understanding, therefore, how to foster emotional resilience becomes not just beneficial but essential to maintain effectiveness in their roles. Emotional resilience, as we will explore, is the ability for a leader to recover quickly from setbacks, adapt well to change, and keep moving forward in the face of adversity, a skill that can be cultivated through specific practices and programs designed to enhance this capacity. One might wonder, what exactly constitutes emotional resilience and why is it so crucial for leaders who are guided by their faith in God?

Firstly, emotional resilience refers to the inner strength that helps individuals handle various stresses and shocks in life, including workplace challenges, personal trials, or unexpected changes. For a leader, this resilience not only helps them to manage their own emotional responses but also sets a powerful example for their teams, demonstrating how challenges should be met with grace and strength. Given the high-pressure environment that leaders often operate in, being able to maintain a positive attitude and a clear mind is indispensable, and it is here that emotional resilience plays a pivotal role.

Good leadership demands consistency in decision-making and actions, which can only be upheld by a leader who does not falter under emotional duress. Programs and practices that foster emotional resilience thus focus on building these capacities, enabling leaders to not overreact to emotional situations but instead respond with calculated and thoughtful actions that align with their core values and the organization's goals. But how, specifically, can emotional resilience be built, and what are the techniques that help maintain a positive attitude even in challenging situations?

To train for emotional resilience, leaders can engage in various exercises that promote a deep understanding of personal emotional triggers and effective methodologies for managing them. Practices such as regular reflective journaling, mindfulness exercises, and structured peer discussion groups can provide substantial benefits. Reflective journaling allows leaders to document their emotional experiences and reflect on them objectively, a practice that helps in recognizing emotional patterns and triggers. Mindfulness exercises, such as meditation or focused breathing, help in calming the mind and reducing the impact of stressors, enabling leaders to maintain clarity in thought and purpose in actions.

Moreover, peer discussion groups serve as a supportive environment where leaders can share their experiences and learn from each other, gaining insights into different methods of handling similar challenges. These groups also offer emotional support, which in itself can strengthen resilience as leaders realize they are not alone in their struggles. All these practices enhance a leader's ability to stay positive and composed, directly impacting their efficacy in leadership roles. When competence in leadership is determined not just by making popular decisions but ones that are aligned with deep-seated beliefs and principles, the importance of emotional resilience becomes all the more clear.

Thus, the sustained effectiveness of leadership amidst the trials and tribulations of both professional and personal life is significantly supported by emotional resilience. It is a quality that is continuously honed and developed through deliberate and consistent practice. By committing to training for emotional resilience, leaders ensure that their capacity to guide, inspire, and maintain their values is never compromised, no matter the emotional challenges they face. Leaders who believe in a higher power often find additional strength in their faith, which can be integrated into resilience-building practices, reinforcing their resolve and providing a higher sense of purpose in their leadership journey.

Indeed, for every leader who holds dear their belief in God, recognizing that their emotional resilience is as much a part of their spiritual journey as it is their professional development can be enlightening. It is not merely about staying strong in the face of adversity but about growing from each experience, guided by their faith and a firm understanding of the purpose they serve. The journey to building and maintaining emotional resilience is ongoing, a path well worth traversing for the profound impact it has on their ability to lead effectively and with a heart full of faith.

Recap and Actionable Steps

Throughout our discussions in this chapter, we have explored the intricate balance between emotions and knowledge, which is a vital aspect of leadership that cannot be overlooked, especially for leaders who are guided by their faith and conviction in God's wisdom. Understanding this balance is not just about recognizing your feelings but also about strategically managing them so they complement, rather than compromise, your decision-making processes. One key aspect we've emphasized is the development of emotional intelligence, which allows leaders to not only handle their own emotions but also to better understand and influence the emotions of others in their team, aligning with the Biblical principle of leading with wisdom and compassion.

To enhance your capabilities as a leader who balances knowledge with emotional insight, it is essential to adopt practices that foster both emotional resilience and intelligence. Developing these qualities ensures that your leadership is not swayed by transient emotions but is anchored in a deep understanding of both the facts at hand and the emotional dynamics at play. Now, let us delve into some specific, actionable steps that you can take to cultivate these essential skills in your daily leadership practice, ensuring that each step aligns with your values and beliefs as a leader who serves under God's guidance.

Actionable Steps to Enhance Emotional Intelligence and Resilience

Regular Self-Reflection: Dedicate time each week to reflect on decisions made and the emotions that influenced those decisions. This practice can be as simple as keeping a journal where you not only record what decisions were made but also how you felt at the time, what triggered those feelings, and how you managed them. Over time, this will help you identify patterns in your emotional responses and better understand how they influence your leadership.

Emotional Awareness Exercises: Engage in daily exercises that boost your awareness of your emotional state. This could involve mindfulness practices, meditation, or prayer, where you focus solely on identifying your current emotional state without trying to change it. By becoming more aware of your emotions, you can begin to manage them more effectively, ensuring they do not overwhelm your ability to lead with clarity and purpose.

Seek Feedback: Regularly ask for feedback from trusted colleagues, mentors, or counselors about how your emotions appear to influence your leadership style. This feedback can provide you with an external perspective on your emotional impact, helping you to adjust your behavior in ways that might not be obvious to you from an internal perspective.

Training and Workshops: Participate in workshops or training sessions that focus on developing emotional intelligence. These programs often provide practical tools and techniques that can enhance your ability to understand and manage not only your emotions but also those of your team members.

Factual Reassessment: When faced with a decision, make it a practice to reassess the facts before finalizing your judgment. This step is crucial in ensuring that your decisions are not solely based on emotional reactions but are supported by factual evidence and rationality. It helps maintain a balance between what you feel and what you know, aligning with the objective of leading wisely as taught in Proverbs.

Encourage Open Communication: Foster an environment where team members feel safe to express their emotions and thoughts. Open communication can demystify the emotional landscape of your team, allowing you to lead more effectively by addressing the needs and concerns of your team members as they arise.

By integrating these steps into your leadership practice, you not only enhance your own emotional intelligence and resilience but also model these qualities for your team. This modeling is critical as it sets a standard in your organization for handling emotions in a healthy, constructive way, thereby enhancing overall team effectiveness and cohesion. Remember, leadership is not just about making good decisions; it's about making those decisions in a way that is respectful of both the emotional and factual realities of your organization, which is a reflection of the wisdom that comes from a balance of heart and mind.

In conclusion, as leaders who believe in God, it is our responsibility to lead not just with authority but also with empathy, understanding, and resilience. These qualities are not just beneficial—they are essential for leadership that honors God and inspires people. By following the steps outlined above, you can ensure that your leadership is not only effective but also reflective of the divine wisdom that guides your life and work.

Know the Difference Between Local Employment and Global Assignment - Purpose

"Then the word of the LORD came unto me, saying, before I formed thee in the belly I knew thee; and before thou camest forth out of the womb I sanctified thee, and I ordained thee a prophet unto the nations." Jeremiah 1:4-5 Your purpose is OLDER than your age! Your purpose is bigger than your location.

Problems and Context

In the life of every leader who believes in God, there comes a moment when the need to understand one's own calling becomes paramount, especially when juxtaposed against the day-to-day realities of local employment responsibilities and the broader, more expansive vision of having a global impact. It's not just about doing a job; it's about fulfilling a purpose that aligns with one's divine call, a purpose that often stretches beyond the immediate scope of local duties and into the wider world which God loves and cares for deeply. Leaders, in their striving to embody this divine directive, frequently encounter the fundamental challenge of aligning local roles with global objectives, a task that is as daunting as it is critical, for the alignment is not merely a matter of logistical arrangement but of spiritual and vocational significance.

This alignment is deeply rooted in the understanding that a leader's local role is not just a job but a platform, a divinely appointed position from which to influence, shape, and participate in a larger global narrative. However, the most challenging aspect arises when, despite a clear calling and global vision, the current employment seems limited, confined, or even in opposition to this broader purpose. It is in these moments that a leader might feel their employment is in limbo, caught between the practicalities of their job and the spiritual impetus of their call. This limbo, far from being a mere professional inconvenience, can often feel like a profound personal trial, testing one's faith, resilience, and ability to discern God's will in complex circumstances.

The difficulties leaders face in such scenarios are not just about managing tasks or responsibilities; they are about nurturing and preserving the essence of their calling amidst the pressures and constraints of local roles. It becomes imperative, then, to not only recognize but actively address these challenges, to seek ways to ensure that one's local engagement does not merely survive but thrives in synchronization with one's global aspirations. This thriving is essential not only for the leader's personal and spiritual fulfillment but also for the broader impact they are meant to have on the world, an impact that transcends geographic and cultural boundaries, resonating with the universal nature of their divine mission.

Consequently, this section aims to delve deep into these challenges, providing clear, actionable insights that leaders can implement to harmonize their local responsibilities with their global vision effectively. It is about equipping leaders with the necessary tools, perspectives, and strategies to turn potential points of friction into opportunities for growth and impactful leadership. By addressing these issues head-on, leaders are better prepared to navigate the complexities of their roles, ensuring that their local presence is not just maintained but is dynamically integrated with their global vision, thus fulfilling their purpose in a manner that is both locally effective and globally significant.

Defining Your Local Responsibilities

When you, as a leader who deeply believes in God, look at your role in the context of your local environment, you see a field where your direct influence and actions can manifest visibly and swiftly; this is the ground where the seeds of your leadership take root, and it is imperative to understand thoroughly what this entails in order to nurture them into flourishing outcomes. The clarity with which you define your local roles and responsibilities sets the foundational bedrock upon which you can build not only your personal success but also the collective success of your community, fostering an atmosphere where both local prosperity and global aspirations can thrive in a harmonious balance. This venture starts with a deep dive into the specific duties you are expected to fulfill – these range from managing your team effectively, ensuring projects align with the broader mission of the organization, to more nuanced roles such as being a moral and ethical guide to your peers and subordinates.

Striving to excel in these local settings requires a blend of practical strategies and a clear vision that aligns with your spiritual and professional values; it is about making the most of the resources at hand, optimizing processes and ensuring that every team member feels valued and motivated. Remember, the effectiveness with which you handle these local responsibilities directly impacts your ability to influence on a larger scale, which is why it is crucial to master the art of local leadership first. One practical strategy to achieve excellence in your local environment is regular and open communication with your team, fostering an environment where feedback is sought and valued, and where each member feels they have the support and guidance needed to excel in their roles. Additionally, setting clear, achievable goals for each project and maintaining a transparent, ethical approach to leadership can significantly enhance your effectiveness as a local leader.

However, it is not uncommon to feel the weight of personal challenges and pains amidst your public success; sometimes, these personal struggles can anchor you, making it seem difficult to focus on or prioritize your responsibilities. It is in these moments that your faith and leadership philosophy are tested the most, and it is also when they can shine the brightest. Embracing these challenges as part of your journey and using them to strengthen your resolve and deepen your compassion can transform potential setbacks into powerful testimonies of resilience and dedication. This process involves acknowledging the difficulties without allowing them to define or derail your mission, seeking support when necessary, and continually returning to your core values and purpose for guidance and strength.

One must also remember the balancing act that lies in aligning these local demands with your aspirations for global impact, which can seem daunting but is integral to developing a truly comprehensive leadership approach. Techniques for maintaining this balance include prioritizing tasks based on their alignment with both local and global objectives, delegating effectively to ensure local operations run smoothly even as you engage with broader initiatives, and continually educating yourself and your team about global trends and needs, integrating this knowledge into your local strategies. By applying these techniques, you can create a synergistic dynamic where local success feeds into global ambitions, and vice versa, each aspect of your leadership reinforcing and elevating the other.

At the core of all these efforts is the understanding that your work, though grounded in local soil, reaches far beyond its immediate boundaries, touching lives and shaping futures in ways you may never fully see but that are nonetheless profound. It is a calling of great responsibility and even greater potential, where each decision you make and each action you take can ripple outward, contributing to a tapestry of change and growth that spans communities and crosses borders. By defining and excelling in your local responsibilities, not only do you set the stage for broader impact, but you also exemplify the kind of leadership that is rooted in integrity, driven by purpose, and expansive in its reach, a true testament to the power of faith-guided leadership in making a difference both at home and around the world.

Expanding Vision to Global Impact

When you, as a leader who believes in the guidance and providence of God, start to think beyond the borders of your immediate environment, you begin a journey that not only broadens your influence but also deepens your understanding of what it means to serve and lead in a world that is incredibly interconnected; this realization is crucial for anyone who aspires to make a difference on a global scale, where the challenges are vast but the opportunities for impact are even greater. It is essential to recognize that expanding your vision to include global considerations isn't just about physical presence in different locales but about fostering a mindset that consistently acknowledges and addresses the needs and potentials of diverse populations, thereby aligning your local commitments with the broader, international picture which ultimately reflects a holistic approach to leadership that resonates with the values you cherish as a believer.

One of the fundamental techniques to enhance your capability to lead on a global scale is to actively develop cultural competency, which involves more than just an awareness of differences in customs or languages; it is about cultivating a deep respect and understanding of various cultural perspectives and values, thereby enabling you to communicate effectively and empathetically across diverse groups. This skill not only aids in reducing potential conflicts but also significantly improves the effectiveness of your leadership by ensuring that all voices are heard and valued, particularly in a global setting where the complexity of issues demands a multifaceted approach that respects and integrates diverse viewpoints. Therefore, it becomes not just beneficial but essential to engage in continuous learning and exposure to different cultures, which can be achieved through various means such as collaborative international projects, attending global conferences, or simply fostering a diverse team environment where different cultural backgrounds are represented and celebrated.

Moreover, the idea that to be absent locally is to be present globally highlights an important aspect of global leadership, where sometimes, focusing on broader, international goals might require you to delegate your local responsibilities effectively; this doesn't mean neglecting your local duties but rather understanding that your role as a leader isn't confined to direct, hands-on involvement in every local issue but can also be about guiding, inspiring, and setting up systems that ensure your local team can operate effectively even in your physical absence. By setting up strong, responsible leadership practices and clear communication channels at the local level, you empower your team to handle day-to-day operations, which frees you up to focus on broader strategic goals that have global implications, thus ensuring that your impact is both deep and wide, reaching beyond immediate geographical boundaries to touch lives and make a difference on a global scale.

Finally, developing a global mindset while fulfilling local duties is not about choosing one over the other but about integrating both perspectives into your leadership vision; it's about understanding that what happens in a local context can have far-reaching effects and vice versa. Strategies for fostering this integrated mindset include regular reviews of how local actions align with global strategies, being open to adopting international best practices that can be localized effectively, and always being keen to learn from the global impacts of local decisions. This holistic view not only enhances your leadership effectiveness but also positions you as a visionary leader who understands the complexities and interdependencies of our globalized world, making you better equipped to face the challenges of leadership in the 21st century with wisdom, compassion, and effectiveness that transcends borders.

Aligning Local and Global Goals

In the journey of leadership, especially when you hold the mantle and believe in a higher calling, it is vital that you align your local responsibilities with the overarching global missions of your organization; this is a challenge that carries a weight of immense responsibility and requires a thoughtful approach, one that seamlessly integrates small-scale actions into the grand tapestry of global strategies. When a leader manages to create harmony between local actions and global objectives, it sets a powerful example and motivates teams to perform with a unified vision, but achieving this alignment is far from straightforward and demands a comprehensive understanding and meticulous planning.

One effective method to ensure that local actions are not just fulfilling immediate needs but are also contributing towards the global goals is to incorporate global perspectives right from the planning stage of local projects; this means that when you, as a leader, sit down to strategize on local initiatives, you consciously factor in how these initiatives can serve broader global purposes. For instance, if a local project involves developing a new product or service, consider how this can address not just local market needs but also how it can be adapted or scaled to meet global market demands or how it can advance the organization's global branding and positioning.

Moreover, another technique to foster this alignment is through regular communication of the global vision to your local teams; this isn't just about sending emails or making announcements about global strategies, but about deeply engaging your team in understanding why global goals matter and how their contributions are vital. It is about creating dialogues, perhaps through workshops or team meetings, where global objectives are discussed in detail, and team members are invited to explore how their work connects to these larger aims. By doing so, you help to cultivate a team that is not only aware of the global objectives but is also committed to achieving them.

Additionally, integrating global perspectives into local decision-making can significantly enhance the alignment process; this involves considering global trends, market conditions, and international standards when making decisions at the local level. For example, when deciding on supplier selection or sourcing materials, you might opt for options that, while perhaps not the most cost-effective locally, align better with the global sustainability goals of your organization, thereby supporting broader initiatives such as reducing environmental impact or enhancing the brand's reputation for social responsibility on a global scale.

Finally, another strategy to synchronize local and global objectives involves revising and adapting local systems and processes to better support the execution of global strategies; this could mean upgrading technology systems to ensure they are compatible with those used by other branches worldwide, or it might involve training local staff with skills that are in demand globally within your organization, thus preparing your team not just to excel in local markets but to contribute effectively to global needs as well. Therefore, by taking these steps, you ensure that every local effort not only meets immediate needs but also propels your organization toward its global ambitions, making every small step part of a much bigger journey towards achieving a harmonious and impactful global presence.

Each of these techniques offers a pathway to ensure that every decision made at the local level not only serves immediate needs but also aligns with and enhances global strategies, creating a cohesive and dynamic environment where local and global objectives support and amplify each other. Thus, as a leader who believes in a greater purpose, it is your responsibility to bridge the gap between local actions and global visions, ensuring that your leadership not only meets the immediate needs of the communities and markets you serve locally but also furthers the broader missions of your organization on the global stage.

Managing Conflicts Between Local and Global Objectives

When a leader who believes in a higher purpose faces the challenge of balancing local and global objectives, it becomes not just a managerial task but a mission of alignment between immediate responsibilities and expansive visions; it is here that strategies to resolve conflicts and leverage synergies between these often competing demands come to play an essential role in leadership effectiveness. One of the first methods to consider in this balancing act is the clear identification and understanding of where these conflicts arise, which typically occurs when the immediate needs of local operations seem to clash with the broader goals set on a global scale, leading to a situation where decisions are not merely administrative but deeply linked to strategic vision and ethical leadership.

Training and resources form the backbone of equipping leaders with the necessary tools to navigate these dual-focused roles, where it is crucial to understand that knowledge is as much about depth as it is about breadth; comprehensive training programs should therefore not only address specific skills such as negotiation, communication, and strategic decision-making but also foster a deep understanding of cultural nuances and global market dynamics, thereby preparing leaders to think globally even when acting locally. Furthermore, these training programs should be designed as continuous learning journeys, adapting to the ever-changing global landscape, ensuring leaders are always equipped with the most relevant and impactful strategies.

Another effective method for managing these conflicts involves prioritizing between local and global demands, a process that requires a meticulous evaluation of the impacts of decisions at both levels; leaders must develop the ability to foresee potential consequences of local actions on global goals and vice versa, using a prioritized approach that aligns with the overall purpose and mission of the organization. This prioritization often requires difficult choices and sacrifices; however, when done correctly, it not only resolves the immediate conflicts but also strengthens the organization's ability to achieve long-term success on a global scale.

Techniques for creating win-win solutions in situations where local and global objectives conflict are critical as these techniques foster an environment of cooperation and mutual benefit, which in turn enhances the overall cohesion within the organization. One such technique is the integration of local insights into global strategies, where local leaders contribute their on-ground experiences and challenges into the global decision-making process, thereby ensuring that global strategies are not only inclusive but also practically applicable across diverse geographical regions. This integration not only helps in tailoring global objectives to fit local realities but also empowers local leaders, making them feel valued and an essential part of the organization's global journey.

In conclusion, managing conflicts between local and global objectives is a dynamic and complex aspect of leadership that requires a well-rounded approach encompassing training, prioritization, and innovative conflict resolution techniques. By focusing on these strategies, leaders can ensure that their actions and decisions resonate well both locally and globally, aligning with their belief in a higher purpose and their commitment to ethical leadership. This alignment not only drives organizational success across various dimensions but also contributes profoundly to personal fulfillment as a leader guided by faith and purpose.

Recap and Actionable Steps

After exploring the nuances of balancing local responsibilities with a vision for global impact throughout this chapter, it's essential to synthesize our learning and translate it into concrete, actionable steps that can guide you, as a leader who believes in God, to not only manage but excel in harmonizing these dual aspects of your leadership role.

Firstly, it's crucial to understand that managing both local and global objectives isn't just about juggling tasks; it's about aligning your day-to-day activities with the broader, God-given mission that transcends geographical boundaries. This alignment requires a deep understanding of the specific responsibilities that come with your local role while also embracing the opportunities and challenges of global leadership. Here, your faith can serve as a compass, guiding your decisions and helping you stay true to your spiritual and professional path.

Now, let's delve into some specific, actionable steps you can take to ensure that your leadership effectively bridges local and global contexts:

Begin by clearly defining your local responsibilities and global goals. Write them down in a way that reflects their potential to contribute to both immediate community needs and broader, international objectives. This clarity will help you prioritize tasks and make strategic decisions.

Implement regular reflection and evaluation sessions where you assess how well your local actions align with and contribute to your global objectives. During these sessions, ask yourself critical questions about the impact of your work and make adjustments as necessary. This practice will not only keep your goals aligned but also provide opportunities for spiritual reflection and growth.

Develop cultural competency by engaging with diverse communities and learning from them. This can be achieved through reading, participating in cultural events, or direct community engagement. Understanding diverse perspectives will enhance your ability to make decisions that are respectful and effective across different cultural contexts.

Communicate your global vision to your local team clearly and consistently. Use simple, relatable language to explain how their work contributes to larger goals. This communication should be ongoing and integrated into regular interactions to keep the team motivated and aligned with the global mission.

Finally, foster an environment of continuous learning and adaptation within your team. Encourage them to seek out global perspectives and bring those insights into local projects. This can be facilitated through training programs, guest speakers, or incentivized learning opportunities.

In conclusion, as a leader who holds faith dear, your journey is not just about professional growth, but also about spiritual fulfillment and purpose. Each step taken to synchronize local and global objectives should also be a step towards greater understanding and service to God's plan. Remember, your role is pivotal in bridging the gap between immediate community needs and broader, global aspirations, making your leadership a powerful conduit for change and impact.

By following these steps, you not only enhance your effectiveness as a leader but also deepen your spiritual journey, finding greater purpose in your day-to-day responsibilities. Such integration not only fulfills organizational goals but also contributes to a higher, divine calling, enriching both your life and those of the people you lead.

Know When It's Personal and When It's Purposeful - Conviction

"But as for you, ye thought evil against me; but God meant it unto good, to bring to pass, as it is this day, to save much people alive. Genesis 50:20.

Blessed are the flexible, for they shall not be bent out of shape."

Problems and Context

It can indeed prove to be quite a challenging task to distinguish between when decisions are driven by personal emotions and when they are inspired by a clear-cut professional purpose, particularly when you are in a leadership position and every move you make is under scrutiny; this scrutiny is not just from your peers but also from your own conscience, which, as a leader who believes in God, you strive to keep as pure and unbiased as possible.

The essence of professional integrity lies in making decisions that are not only effective but are also impartial and fair, a standard that becomes difficult to uphold when personal biases start to cloud judgment; imagine the impact on your team's motivation and trust in leadership if they start feeling that decisions are being made not on the basis of merit or organizational need, but personal preference or prejudice, thus undermining the very foundation on which effective leadership stands.

There is a particular truth in the saying that sometimes '1% defines 99%', which in the context of leadership means that sometimes a single, seemingly small, subjective decision can cast a shadow over the other 99% of your decisions that are objective and well-intentioned; this is why as leaders, especially leaders who operate within a framework of faith and conviction, it is crucial to be vigilant about the origins of our decisions, ensuring they are not just a one-way street that leads back to our personal biases or unresolved emotions.

What complicates things further is that as human beings, our lives and experiences shape our perceptions, which in turn can influence our professional roles in subtle ways; this intertwining of personal emotions and professional responsibilities, if not carefully managed, can lead to choices that might not only affect our effectiveness as leaders but can also impact our personal spiritual peace and professional integrity, therefore, understanding the distinction and maintaining a balance becomes not just a professional requirement but a moral imperative as well.

As leaders who are guided by their faith in God, the challenge is to navigate these waters with both wisdom and humility, constantly seeking divine guidance to ensure that our personal feelings do not overshadow our professional judgments, thereby ensuring that our actions are always in alignment with both divine will and professional ethics, thus maintaining the delicate balance between being human and being a leader.

To effectively manage this balance, it is essential to develop a keen self-awareness that can help in recognizing when our personal feelings are beginning to influence our professional decisions; this self-awareness, coupled with a steadfast commitment to ethical leadership, can significantly enhance our ability to make decisions that are not only just and fair but are also reflective of our convictions as leaders who believe in and are guided by a higher power, thus making every decision not just a professional or personal one, but a purposeful one that serves a greater good.

In conclusion, as leaders in faith, our journey must be one of constant self-evaluation and adherence to both divine principles and professional standards, ensuring that our leadership is not just effective but also righteous and true to the values we cherish; this journey, while challenging, is also immensely rewarding as it allows us to lead with both conviction and compassion, making a difference in the world not just through our professional achievements but through our moral and spiritual contributions as well.

Identifying Personal Bias

As leaders who hold faith and leadership in high regard, recognizing the subtle yet significant ways that personal biases can creep into decision-making is essential, not only for our integrity but also for the effectiveness of our leadership in the organizations we serve. When we discuss tools to recognize these biases, we're diving into a toolkit that includes reflective practices, feedback mechanisms, and structured decision-making processes that ensure our actions align with our true purpose and not merely our personal preferences. Self-awareness, a fundamental attribute of great leaders, grows stronger when we reflect on our decisions and question the influence of our biases in them, thereby enhancing our professional integrity.

Indeed, there are moments in leadership when despite our best efforts, our contributions might seem null and void due to unrecognized biases influencing our decisions; this is a critical point of learning and growth for any leader. It is here that we must pause and consider whether our decisions are driven by what is best for the organization or by our personal viewpoints. Techniques to distinguish between personal preferences and organizational needs include actively seeking out diverse perspectives and employing decision-making frameworks that prioritize organizational goals over personal inclinations, ensuring that our leadership faithfully supports the wider mission of our organizations rather than our individual perspectives.

By consistently applying these techniques and tools, we not only make decisions that are more aligned with our organizational needs but also foster a culture of trust, respect, and integrity. This process is invaluable in leadership as it allows us to serve our organizations and followers more effectively, fulfilling the higher purpose to which we are called by our faith and leadership roles. The journey toward overcoming personal biases is ongoing and requires continuous commitment and vigilance; however, the rewards of such diligence are immeasurable, not only in terms of organizational success but also in our growth as leaders who serve a purpose greater than themselves.

Strategies for Objective Decision Making

As leaders who uphold faith and leadership together, recognizing the vital significance of making decisions based not on personal whims but on solid, undeniable facts and professional standards becomes crucial; this understanding guides our actions and molds our leadership into one that is respected and revered, not just within our circles, but also in the broader community which we serve. Techniques that ensure such decisions can be as straightforward as establishing a clear set of guidelines that delineate the boundaries between personal beliefs and professional duties, thereby allowing decisions to be made with a focus on fairness and efficacy, which is essential in nurturing a trustworthy and effective leadership environment. This act of balancing is not just about ticking boxes, but about genuinely understanding the impact of each decision on the organization's welfare and its stakeholders, which leads us to appreciate the importance of accountability systems in maintaining objectivity.

Accountability systems are not merely there for oversight but are fundamental in providing a framework within which decisions can be evaluated and justified, thus ensuring that every action taken is in the best interest of the organization and not swayed by personal biases; these systems act as a mirror reflecting the true nature of our decisions back at us, urging us to look closely and honestly at our choices. When our participation in decision-making is akin to crossing T's and dotting I's, it implies that our role is pivotal in validating the integrity of the process, reinforcing the need to adhere strictly to established professional standards and facts rather than personal opinions or emotions, which could cloud judgment. This level of diligence ensures that leadership remains robust and just, fostering an environment where every member feels valued and fairly treated, thus enhancing overall organizational morale and productivity.

Furthermore, methods for gathering and analyzing objective data for decision-making are indispensable tools that assist leaders in making informed decisions; this involves collecting data systematically, using tools and techniques that ensure the data's relevance and accuracy, followed by a rigorous analysis to derive actionable insights that genuinely reflect the needs and opportunities facing the organization. This process requires a meticulous approach where every piece of data is scrutinized and its implications fully understood, thereby allowing leaders to make decisions that are not only timely but are also backed by concrete evidence, which fortifies the leader's credibility and the organization's strategic direction. This meticulous approach to decision-making, rooted in objectivity, ensures that the decisions made are defensible and aligned with the organization's long-term goals, thereby fostering stability and growth.

Implementing these strategies within your leadership framework transforms the very essence of decision-making from a task often clouded by personal biases into a disciplined, objective, and systematic process; such transformation is not just beneficial but essential in today's fast-paced and complex organizational landscapes where every decision can have wide-ranging implications. By adhering to these strategies, leaders not only enhance their effectiveness but also model a caliber of leadership that is grounded in integrity and fairness, inspiring others within the organization to uphold these valuable principles as well. This ripple effect of positive leadership practices enhances the entire organization's performance and reputation, ultimately leading to sustained success and fulfillment of the organization's mission and vision.

In conclusion, embracing these strategies for objective decision-making and embedding them into the core of our leadership practice serves not only to enhance the quality of decisions made but also elevates the moral and ethical standards of the organization. As leaders who are guided by both faith and a commitment to excellence, it is our duty to ensure that every decision, no matter how small, reflects the values we cherish and the professionalism we strive to embody. This commitment to objective and principled decision-making is what distinguishes truly transformational leaders from the rest, setting a benchmark for others to aspire to, and creating a legacy of integrity and success that transcends our tenure.

Balancing Personal Ethics with Professional Roles

In the life of a leader who holds their faith and convictions dear, the journey of aligning personal beliefs with professional responsibilities often presents itself as a delicate dance, one that requires not only keen awareness but also a steadfast commitment to integrity; as leaders, the challenge is to integrate personal ethics in a manner that doesn't just coexist with but actually enhances professional decision-making, ensuring that every action taken and decision made under your leadership not only aligns with but also elevates the ethical standards of your organization.

Understanding the role of ethical leadership in fostering an environment of trust and respect is paramount; this is not just about making decisions that are right in the eyes of the law or beneficial from a business perspective, but about making decisions that are also right in the eyes of God and reflective of the values you hold dear, which in turn cultivates a culture where trust and respect flourish among team members and stakeholders alike, creating a ripple effect of positive outcomes that extend beyond the immediate business objectives to impact the broader community in profound ways.

Consider the moments when the outer man is hurting, and yet the inner man is at peace; these moments are indicative of the complex scenarios where professional pressures and personal beliefs might not initially seem to align, presenting leaders like yourself with decisions that could be unsettling on a personal level yet necessary from a professional standpoint, and it is here that your ethical compass must guide you, helping you navigate these waters with grace and conviction, ensuring that your actions not only meet the required standards but also contribute positively to your personal integrity and spiritual wellbeing.

In dealing with such challenging professional situations, the strategies for maintaining personal integrity become not just useful but essential; these strategies might include regular reflection on one's values, seeking counsel from trusted advisors who share your ethical viewpoints, or even engaging in prayerful consideration of the impacts of your decisions, all of which can serve as anchors that keep your professional actions aligned with your personal ethics, ensuring that you remain steadfast in your convictions while effectively fulfilling your leadership role.

The integration of personal ethics into professional roles is not a one-time act but a continuous process of alignment and realignment, especially as new situations arise and the business landscape evolves; it requires ongoing attention and intentionality to ensure that your personal beliefs do not just inform but actively enhance your professional decisions, leading to outcomes that are beneficial not only for the business and its stakeholders but also in alignment with your spiritual life, thereby ensuring that your leadership is not only effective but also righteous and true to your faith.

In conclusion, as a leader who believes in God, your challenge and indeed your opportunity is to weave your personal ethics seamlessly into your professional roles in a way that they enhance rather than hinder your decision-making processes; this not only sets a standard of ethical leadership within your organization but also serves as a testament to your faith and commitment to living out your beliefs, thereby inspiring those around you to also seek alignment between their personal ethics and professional actions, ultimately leading to a work environment where integrity and respect are the cornerstones of all business dealings.

Preventing Personal Feelings from Overruling Professionalism

In the complex journey of leadership, the challenge often lies not just in making decisions, but in making sure these decisions aren't clouded by our personal feelings, which is a very important concept to grasp because it can significantly influence the integrity and effectiveness of our professional roles. To start, one of the most effective preventative measures to ensure that personal feelings do not compromise professional decisions is to establish clear, well-defined policies that set the standard for decision-making within your organization; these policies act as a roadmap, guiding leaders by providing a framework within which decisions should be made, ensuring that these decisions align with the organization's goals and not with personal biases or emotions.

Furthermore, training plays a crucial role in equipping leaders with the skills needed to maintain professional integrity in the face of personal feelings. By engaging in regular training sessions focused on emotional intelligence and decision-making, leaders can develop the ability to recognize their emotional responses and understand how these might influence their decision-making, thereby learning techniques to separate feelings from professional duties, which is essential because it helps maintain a clear boundary between personal emotions and professional responsibilities. Emotional intelligence training helps leaders to identify their emotions, understand the triggers behind these emotions, and learn strategies to manage them effectively, ensuring that decisions are made based on rational thought rather than emotional impulses.

Another significant technique involves the cultivation of an environment where revelations—deep insights into one's behaviors and the consequences thereof—are encouraged and valued. This involves creating a culture of openness and honesty where leaders can discuss and reflect on how personal feelings might be impacting their professional judgement without fear of judgment or retribution. By fostering such an environment, organizations empower their leaders to gain deeper insights into their own emotional processes and how these might be interfering with their roles, which is instrumental because when leaders understand the impact of their emotions, they can make more conscious choices that favor professional integrity over personal sentiment.

Maintaining professional composure in emotionally charged situations is perhaps one of the most direct ways to prevent personal feelings from overruling professionalism. Techniques such as mindfulness, stress management exercises, and regular reflection can be immensely helpful. Mindfulness techniques, for example, train leaders to stay present and focused, reducing the likelihood of emotional reactions clouding their judgment. Stress management exercises, such as deep breathing or progressive muscle relaxation, help leaders maintain calmness in stressful situations, ensuring that their decisions are guided by a clear and composed mind. Regular reflection sessions, where leaders can contemplate their decisions and the motivations behind them, also play a critical role in helping leaders to recognize patterns in their behavior that may be influenced by personal feelings, allowing them to address these patterns constructively.

Leaders must remember that every decision they make not only impacts their immediate team but can also resonate throughout the entire organization. This is why adopting these techniques and integrating them into everyday leadership practices is not just beneficial but essential for sustaining professional standards and integrity. By prioritizing these practices, leaders not only safeguard their decision-making process from the interference of personal feelings but also set a strong example for others within the organization, thereby fostering a culture of professionalism and integrity that can significantly enhance organizational performance and trust.

Recap and Actionable Steps

Throughout our journey in this chapter, we have traversed the delicate terrain where personal feelings often intersect with professional decisions, a common challenge faced by leaders who strive to act under God's guidance and maintain their integrity in leadership roles. It's essential for you, as a leader with deep convictions, to discern between personal biases and the overarching goals of your organization, ensuring that every decision you make not only aligns with professional standards but also resonates with your spiritual values. This balance is crucial, not just for the success of your organization but for your personal spiritual journey and fulfillment as a leader.

To assist you in this endeavor, let's consolidate the key insights we've covered and translate these into actionable, straightforward steps that you can implement to ensure your decisions are both objective and infused with your personal ethics. By following these steps, you will enhance your ability to make decisions that are not only effective but also reflect your deep-seated beliefs and convictions, fostering an environment of trust and respect among your colleagues and subordinates.

Firstly, it's imperative to establish a routine of self-reflection and bias-checking that can guide your decision-making process. This can be accomplished through the following detailed steps:

Daily Reflection: Begin each day with a prayer or meditation session focused on seeking clarity and guidance. Use this time to ask for the strength to recognize and set aside personal biases that might cloud your judgment.

Maintain a Decision Journal: Keep a record of significant decisions you make, detailing the reasons behind each decision and the values or biases that influenced these reasons. Regularly review this journal to identify patterns in your decision-making that may indicate recurring biases.

Seek Diverse Perspectives: Before finalizing a decision, consult with a diverse group of trusted advisors who can provide alternative viewpoints and challenge your preconceptions, ensuring that your decisions are well-rounded and consider multiple aspects of a situation.

Implement a Bias-Check Tool: Utilize tools or frameworks designed to detect and correct biases in decision-making. These tools often involve a series of questions that help you examine whether your decision is influenced by personal feelings or professional ethics.

Next, to ensure that your decisions are objective and professionally sound, it's crucial to integrate systematic checks and balances into your decision-making process:

Establish Clear Guidelines: Develop and adhere to a set of criteria for decision-making that aligns with your organization's goals and your personal ethics. These guidelines should serve as a benchmark to measure the objectivity of your decisions.

Use Data-Driven Analysis: Whenever possible, base your decisions on data and factual analysis rather than personal intuition. This approach helps minimize the influence of personal bias and increases the likelihood of achieving unbiased outcomes.

Regular Accountability Checks: Schedule regular reviews of your decisions with your accountability partners or mentors. These checks should focus on evaluating the adherence to your established decision-making criteria and the outcomes of your decisions.

Finally, to maintain your conviction and incorporate your personal ethics into your professional responsibilities effectively, consider these steps:

Align Actions with Values: Regularly revisit your personal and organizational values to ensure that your actions and decisions are in harmony with these principles. This alignment is essential for maintaining your integrity and the trust of those you lead.

Continuous Learning: Commit to ongoing education about ethical leadership and decision-making. Attend workshops, seminars, or courses that can enhance your understanding and application of ethics in your professional role.

Practice Resilience: In moments of ethical dilemmas, stand firm in your convictions and be prepared to defend your ethical decisions. This resilience not only tests your commitment to your values but also sets a powerful example for your team.

By meticulously following these actionable steps, you will strengthen your ability to separate personal feelings from professional duties, thereby enhancing your effectiveness as a leader who operates under the guidance of God. This comprehensive approach ensures that your leadership is not only successful in achieving business objectives but also in fulfilling a higher spiritual purpose, which is paramount for you as a leader who believes in the profound impact of integrating faith and wor

Know When It's Stress and When It's Strategy - Self-Care

"And Moses' father in law said unto him, The thing that thou doest is not good. Thou wilt surely wear away, both thou, and this people that is with thee: for this thing is too heavy for thee; thou art not able to perform it thyself alone. It surely wear away, both thou, and this people that is with thee: for this thing is too heavy for thee; thou art not able to perform it thyself alone. Hearken now unto my voice, I will give thee counsel, and God shall be with thee: Be thou for the people to God-ward, that thou mayest bring the causes unto God." Exodus 18:17-19

Problems and Context

When you are leading, whether it's a team, a project, or an entire company, the stakes are always high, and it feels like every decision is a critical one. This constant high-stakes environment can lead to a significant amount of stress, which, if not managed properly, can impact not just your health, but the strategic outcomes you are working so hard to achieve. It's important to recognize that managing stress is not just about feeling better on a personal level but is a critical component of effective strategic leadership. When stress levels are high, it can cloud your judgment, make you react rather than respond, and ultimately lead to decisions that might not align with your long-term strategic goals.

Moreover, the consequences of not managing stress effectively can be far-reaching. Poor stress management can lead to burnout, strained relationships within your team, and could even affect your reputation as a leader, making stakeholders lose confidence in your capabilities. This is why it's crucial to embed effective stress management practices not just in your personal routine but also in your strategic planning processes. When leaders are stressed, they tend to focus on short-term firefighting rather than long-term strategic planning, which can steer the entire team or organization away from its objectives.

Your worldview—how you see the world and your place in it—plays a significant role in how you manage stress. If you view stressful situations as threats, your body's natural response can lead to anxiety and panic. However, if you view them as challenges that you are capable of overcoming, it can lead to increased motivation and energy to tackle the problem. This shift in perspective is crucial in managing your responses to stress and aligning them with your strategic goals. It's not just about managing stress but managing how you perceive and react to stress that defines your success as a strategic leader.

Finally, it's important to acknowledge that there is often a discrepancy between what we know intellectually and how we feel emotionally. You might know that a certain amount of stress is normal and can even be beneficial, pushing us to meet deadlines and achieve goals, but that doesn't always make it easier to handle emotionally. Recognizing and addressing this gap between knowledge and feeling is key to developing effective stress management strategies that support your strategic objectives. When leaders align their emotional responses with their intellectual understanding, they set themselves and their teams up for success.

Understanding these dynamics is the first step towards developing a more strategic approach to stress management, which will not only enhance your well-being but will also reinforce the effectiveness of your leadership during tough periods. This understanding helps leaders to not just survive, but thrive in high-pressure environments, turning potential stress into a strategic advantage.

Recognizing Stressors in Leadership Roles

When we talk about leadership, it's essential to recognize that being in charge also involves facing various stressors that can significantly impact your ability to make strategic decisions, and this recognition is the first crucial step towards effective leadership and personal well-being. Leaders often encounter specific challenges that can provoke stress, such as high-stakes decision making, the responsibility for team outcomes, and the constant need to balance personal and professional life; understanding these specific stressors is vital because it allows for the identification of what aspects of your day-to-day activities are contributing to your stress levels. Techniques for the early detection and management of stress are tremendously beneficial, and they start with the simple act of self-observation, where you take a moment each day to reflect on what situations are causing you the most anxiety or discomfort, thereby allowing you to address these issues before they escalate into something unmanageable.

Furthermore, it is not uncommon for leaders to experience a disconnection between their inner voice—how they feel internally about their decisions and actions—and the outer voice, or how they project their decisions and actions to those they lead; recognizing when these two voices are not aligned is essential as it can be an indicator of underlying stress that might be overlooked otherwise. The ability to distinguish between productive pressure, which can motivate you to achieve optimal performance, and harmful stress, which can degrade your health and hinder your performance, is a skill that needs to be developed over time through consistent self-awareness and regulatory practices. Methods to make this distinction clearer involve setting clear and achievable goals, regular consultation with mentors or peers for perspective, and maintaining a healthy lifestyle that supports mental clarity and emotional resilience.

Effective leadership is not just about making tough decisions and inspiring others; it is also about managing your own mental and emotional health so you can remain clear-headed and capable of dealing with whatever challenges come your way. In this light, leaders must adopt a proactive approach to stress management, integrating techniques such as mindfulness, regular physical activity, adequate rest, and balanced nutrition into their daily routine, not only to preserve their health but also to set a positive example for their teams. Ultimately, recognizing and addressing the stressors inherent in leadership roles involves a commitment to self-care and the understanding that maintaining your well-being is just as important as any strategic decision you make for your organization.

Integrating Stress Management into Strategic Planning

In the realm of leadership, where every decision can ripple into success or upheaval, integrating stress management into strategic planning isn't just beneficial; it is fundamentally crucial for maintaining a clear-headed approach to both daily tasks and long-term objectives, as the ability to discern between pressing concerns and unnecessary worries can drastically shape the trajectory of an organization's journey towards its goals. Understanding how to weave effective stress management techniques into the fabric of organizational strategy is not merely about preventing stress but rather about creating a resilient framework that stands robust against the inevitable pressures that accompany leadership roles. It's about shaping a culture where balance is not an afterthought but a baseline from which all operations proceed.

Leaders often find themselves at the helm of their ship in stormy waters, where every wave of decision-making carries the potential to either steer clear of hazards or to crash upon the unseen rocks; here, the role of stress management becomes not just a personal tool, but a strategic asset. Embedding proactive stress management within the planning phase of any project or strategic initiative enables the organization to not only anticipate potential stress points but also to equip its members with the necessary tools to handle pressure effectively, ensuring that their actions and decisions align with the organization's long-term visions and ethical guidelines. This foresight can greatly enhance the efficacy of strategic outcomes, as it ensures that the team's morale and motivation are safeguarded against the eroding effects of chronic stress, which often leads to burnout and decision fatigue.

When considering how to integrate these practices, leaders should start by identifying the common stress points within their strategies and operational models, which often include tight deadlines, high stakes, and significant interpersonal or interdepartmental dependencies. With these stress points mapped out, the next step is to introduce stress management practices that are both proactive and reactive; proactive measures might include regular training sessions focused on stress reduction techniques, incorporating scheduled breaks for mental health throughout project timelines, and setting realistic expectations on deliverables. Reactive measures, on the other hand, involve creating support systems that can be activated during times of high stress, such as peer support groups, access to counseling services, and open communication channels for expressing concerns and challenges without fear of judgment or retribution.

Furthermore, it is crucial for leaders to lead by example when it comes to managing stress effectively; this involves demonstrating healthy stress management behaviors, such as taking meaningful breaks, openly discussing stress and its impacts, and encouraging a work environment where employees feel valued and heard. By setting a precedent of prioritizing mental health alongside organizational goals, leaders not only enhance their own resilience but also inspire their teams to adopt similar practices, creating a collective strength that permeates the entire organization. This environment encourages a more dynamic and adaptive strategic planning process, where team members feel secure and supported, enabling them to contribute more creatively and enthusiastically to strategic discussions and implementations.

In conclusion, the integration of stress management into strategic planning is a transformative strategy that transcends conventional leadership approaches by embedding emotional and psychological resilience at the core of organizational practices. This approach not only enhances the well-being of the team but also fortifies the organization's capacity to pursue its strategic objectives with vigor and clarity. As leaders, the commitment to incorporating stress management techniques into strategic frameworks is a testament to a forward-thinking, holistic approach to leadership—one that values the human elements of operation as much as the financial and procedural ones, ensuring sustainable success and well-being across all levels of the organization.

Tools and Techniques for Effective Stress Management

In the dynamic realm of leadership, where everyday brings new challenges and high-stress situations are more the rule than the exception, mastering the art of stress management is not just beneficial, it is imperative for maintaining both personal health and professional effectiveness, so let us delve deeply into the myriad of tools and techniques that have proven to be effective in reducing stress among leaders, ensuring that you, as a leader facing these tough periods, have a solid foundation upon which you can build a resilient approach to handling the pressures that come with your role.

One of the first strategies that often gets highlighted in discussions about stress management is the practice of mindfulness, which involves being fully present in the moment, aware of where we are and what we're doing, and not overly reactive or overwhelmed by what's going on around us, so imagine you are in a stressful meeting where the stakes are high, and opinions are clashing; by employing mindfulness, you consciously bring your attention to your breath, helping to center your thoughts and calm your nervous system, thus allowing you to approach the situation with a clearer, more focused mindset, which in turn enhances your ability to make strategic decisions under pressure.

Another highly effective tool for managing stress is physical activity, which not only improves your overall health but also boosts your endorphins, the brain's feel-good neurotransmitters, and it's important to note that you don't need to engage in intense workouts to reap these benefits; regular, moderate activities like walking or yoga can significantly alleviate symptoms of stress and anxiety, and by integrating these activities into your regular schedule, you create a valuable outlet for relieving pressure and restoring your mental clarity, thereby enhancing your ability to lead effectively and handle complex issues with a greater level of calm and insight.

Deep breathing exercises are yet another technique that can be easily integrated into your daily routine, providing an immediate effect in reducing stress, and these exercises involve focusing your attention on slow, deep, and consistent breaths, which helps to slow your heart rate and lower blood pressure, creating a feeling of calm that can help mitigate the immediate symptoms of stress, and the beauty of deep breathing is that it can be practiced anywhere, whether you're in your office, at home, or even in your car, making it a versatile tool that you can turn to in virtually any situation when you feel overwhelmed.

In addition to these individual practices, maintaining a network of support is crucial in managing stress effectively, as this can include colleagues who understand the unique pressures of your role, mentors who can provide guidance based on their own experiences, or even professional counselors who can offer strategies to handle stress, and by cultivating strong relationships and an environment of mutual support, you not only enhance your own resilience but also contribute to a healthier, more productive workplace culture, where stress is managed proactively and not just reactively.

Finally, it is essential to recognize the importance of regular, quality sleep as a cornerstone of effective stress management, for sleep recharges the brain, heals the body, and fortifies virtually every system in the body, and without adequate sleep, everything from your ability to handle stress to your emotional stability can be compromised, so by prioritizing good sleep hygiene—keeping a consistent sleep schedule, creating a restful environment, and avoiding caffeine and electronics before bed—you ensure that you are at your best and most resilient self, ready to face whatever challenges come your way.

By understanding and implementing these tools and techniques, you equip yourself with a robust set of skills that can help manage stress effectively, ensuring that you remain a capable leader who can navigate through tough periods with grace and strategy, and more importantly, you maintain your health and well-being in the process, setting a positive example for those you lead and fostering a work environment where stress is managed intelligently and compassionately.

Ensuring Stress Does Not Derail Strategic Objectives

In the complex world of leadership, where each decision can ripple through an organization, the clarity of mind is not just a benefit, it is a requirement; hence, understanding how to manage stress effectively becomes a cornerstone for maintaining not just personal health, but also professional efficacy, particularly when it comes to making strategic decisions that will shape the future of an organization. Now, it is imperative to establish methods that ensure stress does not cloud judgment or hinder the ability to execute strategies effectively, because when the mind is overwhelmed, it is much harder to focus on the goals and objectives that need attention, leading to delayed projects or poorly made decisions that could have far-reaching negative effects on the overall health of the organization.

One of the first steps in ensuring that stress does not interfere with strategic objectives is to develop and implement policies that support leaders in maintaining their strategic focus even when under pressure; this involves setting up an environment where leaders feel supported and know that they have the resources available to manage their stress effectively. Policies such as mandatory breaks, access to mental health resources, and regular check-ins can create an atmosphere of understanding and support, which not only helps in alleviating stress but also reinforces the company's commitment to the well-being of its leaders, thereby fostering a culture where strategic focus is not lost amidst turbulent times.

Furthermore, it is crucial to have interventions ready for when stress levels begin to peak, interventions that are not merely reactive but proactive, aiming to address stress before it becomes a critical issue that interrupts the workflow and decision-making processes. Such interventions could include training sessions focused on stress management techniques, regular team-building activities that promote a positive work environment, and clear communication channels that encourage leaders to speak openly about their stressors without fear of judgment or repercussions. By having these interventions in place, organizations can ensure that their leaders are not only well-prepared to handle their own stress but are also more adept at leading their teams through stressful periods without losing sight of strategic objectives.

Moreover, emphasizing the importance of rest and its role in maintaining strategic focus is essential; rest should not be viewed as a luxury or a sign of weakness, but rather as a critical component of effective leadership. Leaders who are well-rested are more likely to think clearly, make informed decisions, and manage the pressures that come with their roles with more resilience. Therefore, organizations should encourage leaders to take adequate rest and should look at it as a preventive strategy that helps safeguard the leader's ability to perform under pressure while keeping strategic objectives on track.

In conclusion, by recognizing the profound impact stress can have on strategic decision-making and implementing comprehensive strategies to manage and mitigate stress, leaders can ensure that their ability to perform effectively does not waver, even during challenging times. These strategies, from supportive policies and proactive interventions to a strong emphasis on the necessity of rest, not only help in maintaining the focus on strategic objectives but also contribute to creating a healthier work environment where leaders can thrive even in the face of adversity, making the organization more resilient and better equipped to face future challenges.

Recap and Actionable Steps

In the preceding sections of this chapter, we thoroughly explored how leaders can effectively manage stress without compromising their strategic objectives, and now, as we recap, it's essential to solidify that understanding by pinpointing practical steps that can seamlessly integrate stress management into your leadership routines, ensuring you're not only surviving but also thriving during challenging periods. Let's break down these strategies into clear, actionable steps that you can start implementing from today to reinforce your leadership and maintain your well-being amidst the pressures and responsibilities that come with your role.

To begin with, the first strategy that must be highlighted involves establishing a solid routine that prioritizes your mental and physical health, because only a leader who is in good health can make decisions that are not clouded by stress or fatigue; this involves setting aside specific times daily or weekly for activities that reduce stress, such as exercise, meditation, or even engaging hobbies that disconnect you from work-related thoughts. Designating these times in your schedule not only fosters personal well-being but also sets a precedent for your team, demonstrating that while work is important, managing one's health is equally crucial. Next, we must address the importance of setting boundaries, both personally and professionally, to prevent burnout; this means being clear about when you are available and when you are not, which not only helps in managing your stress but also empowers your team to take initiative and make decisions in your absence, thereby fostering a resilient and proactive organizational culture.

Moreover, another step involves open communication with your team about the importance of stress management, not only for yourself but for them as well; this might involve regular check-ins or establishing an open-door policy where team members feel comfortable discussing their stressors, which promotes a supportive environment and helps in identifying stress points within the team before they escalate into larger issues. Furthermore, integrating stress management strategies into the core strategic planning of your organization is essential; this could mean revising deadlines, reallocating resources, or even adjusting project scopes to ensure that the team's workload is realistic and manageable, which in turn reduces stress levels and aids in achieving strategic objectives more efficiently.

Lastly, it is crucial to continually educate yourself and your team about the signs of excessive stress and the techniques to manage it; this could involve workshops, professional development sessions, or even bringing in experts on stress management and mental health. Continuous education not only helps in recognizing the early signs of stress but also equips you and your team with practical tools to manage stress effectively, ensuring that the entire team can remain focused and productive even during the most demanding periods.

In conclusion, the integration of these actionable steps into your daily and strategic routines as a leader is not just about managing stress but about transforming the way you lead and live. By prioritizing these practices, you're setting up yourself and your team for success, ensuring that stress does not compromise your health or your strategic objectives but instead contributes to a resilient, proactive, and healthy organizational culture. Start today, and step into a role of leadership that recognizes the power of effective stress management and strategic planning working hand in hand.

Establish a self-care routine: Dedicate specific times for activities like exercise or hobbies to manage stress.

Set clear personal and professional boundaries: Communicate your availability to balance workload and prevent burnout.

Promote open communication: Discuss stress management openly with your team to foster a supportive environment.

Integrate stress management into strategic planning: Adjust project scopes and resources to ensure manageable workloads.

Invest in continuous education: Regularly update yourself and your team on stress management techniques and mental health.

Know the Difference Between Those Who Stayed and Those Who Left - Relationships

"They went out from us, but they were not of us; for if they had been of us, they would no doubt have continued with us: but they went out, that they might be made manifest that they were not all of us." 1 John 2:19

Problems and Context

When the winds of organizational change start howling, they don't just shuffle papers and processes; they whip through the corridors where professional relationships reside, these invisible yet vital threads that keep the fabric of a company together, and sometimes, they're frayed or even severed by the gusts of change. Maintaining effective communication and trust during these turbulent times can feel as though we're trying to build a house of cards in a tempest, each attempt to align and balance met with new drafts that test the stability of what we've built. Trust, that delicate and intangible asset, becomes even more elusive when the familiarity and predictability of our working environment are replaced with uncertainty and the unknown.

And yet, it is within this very storm that wisdom, an ever so subtle and quietly powerful force, steps in to lift the veil on our hopes and reveal a clearer vision of what we truly need—not always what we had envisaged, but often what will serve us best in the long run. This wisdom understands the 50/20 principle, the notion that what was meant for harm can, in fact, propel us towards our greater good, a principle that, when grasped, can transform the way we perceive our circumstances and relationships. It is not a simple concept to digest, especially when faced with the discomfort of change, but it is one that holds profound implications for leadership and community within an organization.

It is at this juncture that we must pause, take a deep breath, and begin to dissect, with careful attention, the impact these changes are having on our relationships, asking ourselves the hard but necessary questions. Are we communicating effectively with our colleagues, or are we allowing the white noise of change to drown out our messages? Are we clinging to what was, or are we embracing what could be, with the understanding that some relationships may evolve or even come to a natural end? It requires a delicate dance of discernment, to separate the wheat from the chaff, to recognize what relationships can and should be fortified and which ones may have run their natural course, all the while trying to keep the heart and soul of the team intact.

This is the crossroads where leaders who believe in a higher purpose must stand firm, anchoring themselves in the values that have always guided them yet remaining flexible enough to navigate through the shifting landscape. For the stakes are high, and the outcomes will reverberate far beyond the immediate horizon; the relationships that survive this transition have the potential to become stronger, more authentic, and deeply rooted in a shared vision for the future—one that is shaped not just by goals and objectives, but by a collective resilience and unity that can weather any storm.

Understanding the Dynamics of Organizational Change

When we talk about the dynamics of organizational change, we are referring to the typical patterns and stages that almost every organization goes through when it experiences shifts, such as new leadership, mergers, or even shifts in the market that require an adaptation of business strategies, and understanding these patterns is not just about observing changes, but it involves a deep dive into how these changes can predictably impact the relationships within the organization, which includes understanding the emotions, the potential for conflict, and even the opportunities for growth that arise during these turbulent times. Leaders who are armed with this knowledge are better equipped to steer their organizations towards stability and are more capable of maintaining strong, resilient relationships among their team members, which is critical because relationships form the backbone of any successful organization.

Now, one might wonder why it is so important to map these patterns and stages of change, and the reason is quite straightforward; by understanding these patterns, leaders can predict and therefore better manage the impacts of these changes on relationships within the organization, which is especially important because changes often bring about uncertainty and stress, which can strain even the strongest of relationships. If left unchecked, these strains can become cracks that threaten the very foundation of team dynamics and overall organizational health, making it crucial for leaders to not only recognize the stages of change but to understand them deeply and respond to them thoughtfully, ensuring that the organization not only survives the change but emerges stronger.

Historically, changes in organizations have often been accompanied by what we might call 'the history of pain,' which refers to the difficult adjustments and emotional toll that changes can impose on individuals within the organization, and it is this history that thoughtful leaders must consider when navigating through changes, as ignoring the emotional and psychological impacts of change can lead to a disengaged workforce and a toxic work environment. The history of pain isn't just about the challenges, though; it's also about resilience and the incredible potential for growth and transformation that can arise when these challenges are navigated successfully, turning potential negatives into powerful positives that can drive an organization forward.

Finally, one of the most powerful techniques for leaders during times of change is mapping relationship dynamics, which involves tracking and analyzing how relationships within the organization are affected during transitions. This mapping can help leaders identify which relationships are most at risk, which are thriving, and what actions can be taken to support, repair, or even redefine these relationships during and after the transition. This technique is not just about preserving relationships but about strengthening them, utilizing the change as a catalyst for creating deeper connections and a more cohesive team environment, thereby not only maintaining but enhancing the social fabric of the organization.

Thus, understanding the dynamics of organizational change involves recognizing and responding to the patterns and stages of change, acknowledging and learning from the history of pain, and proactively mapping and managing relationship dynamics, all of which are crucial for any leader who aims to lead their team with wisdom and compassion during times of uncertainty. By mastering these elements, leaders not only safeguard their organization's health during tumultuous periods but also set the stage for greater unity and success in the future.

Strategies to Maintain Relationships During Change

In times of significant changes within an organization, maintaining open communications and trust amongst team members becomes not just a goal but a necessity, which forms the cornerstone of enduring professional relationships that can withstand the inevitable storms of transition; it is crucial, therefore, that every leader who believes in the principles of guidance and stewardship takes proactive steps to ensure that lines of communication remain unblocked and transparent. Communicating openly with your team involves sharing both the good and the difficult news with equal honesty, and it is essential to provide regular updates to help everyone understand the context of the changes, the reasons behind them, and how these changes are expected to benefit the organization in the long run, thus preventing misinformation and the spread of rumors that can lead to insecurities and mistrust. One effective strategy to foster this environment of open communication is to establish regular briefing sessions or 'change forums' where team members can ask questions and express concerns; these forums not only serve as a platform for dissemination of information but also as a valuable feedback loop that can provide insights into the team's sentiment and morale, helping leaders to adjust strategies as necessary.

Apart from just keeping everyone informed, another fundamental aspect of maintaining relationship stability during organizational shifts is the role of transparency, which cannot be overstated; transparency during changes involves more than just sharing plans and updates—it requires a vulnerability from leadership to share the unknowns as well. When leaders are transparent about what is not yet known, it humanizes the process, allowing team members to feel that they are truly part of the journey and not just mere passengers; this level of honesty can remarkably enhance loyalty and commitment, as employees generally feel more valued and secure when they are kept in the loop of both the certainties and uncertainties. Moreover, in maintaining relationship stability, it is beneficial to recognize and support the emotional and professional needs of team members by providing them with access to resources such as counseling and career development sessions, which can help individuals manage their stress and align their career paths with the changing goals of the organization, thus reinforcing their loyalty and commitment to the organizational cause during periods of change.

It is also wise to remember that relationships that sustain are those nurtured with mutual respect and understanding, where every member feels acknowledged and valued; thus, methods to foster loyalty and commitment during times of change must include recognizing and celebrating the contributions of team members. Acknowledgment can be as simple as public recognition in meetings, personalized thank-you notes for efforts during tough times, or more formal rewards systems that align with the company's changing objectives and values. These acts of recognition not only boost morale but also reinforce the behaviors and attitudes that support the organization's new direction. Finally, fostering loyalty and commitment in times of change is an ongoing process that requires consistent effort—it is not enough to initiate these practices only at the start of a change process but rather, they should be part of an ongoing strategy to cultivate and maintain a supportive and resilient work culture.

Thus, as leaders who look to navigate through the complex dynamics of change while keeping faith and trust in God's guidance, it is imperative to apply these strategies with compassion and foresight. By ensuring open, honest communication, maintaining transparency, and recognizing the contributions of your team, you create an environment where professional relationships can thrive despite the challenges posed by change. With these practices, not only is the organizational fabric strengthened, but also it becomes more adaptable to future changes, thereby setting a foundation for sustained success and stability. In conclusion, the journey through organizational change is a shared experience, and by nurturing the relationships within your team with these deliberate and thoughtful strategies, you not only preserve but also enhance the core relational assets of your organization during these transformative times.

Rebuilding Relationships Post-Change

When the dust settles after significant organizational changes, it's not uncommon to find that some professional relationships have become strained or even broken; this phenomenon can occur even among well-intended team members who find themselves swept up in the tide of new policies, shifting roles, or altered strategic directions. In such times, it becomes particularly crucial for leaders, especially those who hold their faith and values close, to step forward with a resolve to mend these fissures, recognizing that the pathway to rebuilding relationships within their teams is not just a matter of corporate necessity but a testament to their commitment to stewardship and compassion, qualities much esteemed in both professional and spiritual realms.

The first step in this process involves acknowledging the impacts that these changes have wrought on personal dynamics and professional interactions; it requires a leader to approach this task with a blend of humility and clarity, ensuring that all team members feel heard and validated in their experiences. This acknowledgment is not merely about listing the changes and noting who might have been upset by them; rather, it is about understanding the emotional and practical toll these changes may have taken on individuals, and conveying genuinely that their feelings and challenges are legitimate and important to address, thereby laying a foundational stone for trust to be rebuilt.

Once acknowledgment is thoroughly addressed, the next phase is facilitating a healing process, which involves creating spaces for open dialogue and fostering an environment where team members can express concerns, share feelings, and discuss apprehensions without fear of judgment or reprisal. This might mean setting up regular check-in meetings, perhaps starting each with a short reflection or prayer to set a tone of unity and purpose, where members can talk about the transition and its personal impact on them. Such meetings not only serve as a platform for emotional expression but also help in identifying specific issues that need to be addressed to move forward.

In addition to these discussions, practical strategies for reengaging disengaged team members are crucial and should be pursued with thoughtful intention; this might include assigning them to new projects that align with their skills and professional aspirations or involving them in decision-making processes where their input and insight can be valued and seen. By reintegrating disengaged members in such a meaningful manner, leaders not only utilize their capabilities for organizational benefit but also send a powerful message of inclusion and appreciation, further healing the wounds left by the initial upheavals.

Lastly, one of the most critical steps in rebuilding relationships post-change is restoring trust, which is the cornerstone of any successful team. Rebuilding trust requires consistency, integrity, and time. Leaders must be consistent in their actions and communication, following through on promises and decisions made during and after the transition. They should operate with complete integrity, ensuring that their actions always align with their words and the values they promote, which is especially significant for those who lead with a faith-based perspective, as it reflects their commitment to living out their beliefs in practical, observable ways. Over time, these efforts coalesce to restore and strengthen trust, ultimately leading to a revitalized team dynamic that can withstand future challenges.

In conclusion, rebuilding relationships within a team after periods of significant change is not just about techniques but about leadership that reflects understanding, care, and a commitment to the values that guide one's life and work. For every leader who believes in the power of their faith and values, this process is not only a professional obligation but a spiritual service, a way to manifest the principles they hold dear in the everyday workings of their organization, thereby not just achieving organizational goals but also fostering a community of support, resilience, and mutual respect.

Leveraging Relationships for Organizational Resilience

In the ever-evolving landscape of organizational management, where change is more the norm than the exception, a leader's ability to foster and maintain strong relationships within the team becomes not just beneficial but essential for the organization's resilience and continuity, especially when you, as a leader, believe in the guiding hand of a higher power, knowing that every interaction holds deeper significance beyond mere professional necessity. Strong relationships within a team do not just happen by accident; they are carefully cultivated through trust, understanding, and mutual respect, principles that are deeply rooted in spiritual values, which guide us toward treating each other with kindness and empathy. This cultivation becomes particularly crucial during times of organizational change, a period typically marked by uncertainty and potential unease among team members, where the strength of existing relationships can significantly determine the team's ability to navigate through these changes smoothly.

Fostering strong relationships within an organization is akin to building a buffer against the shocks of change, where each relationship acts like a resilient wall that supports and upholds the structure through turbulent times. When you as a leader invest time and energy into strengthening these bonds, you are essentially weaving a tighter, more cohesive fabric of interpersonal connections that can hold the organization together against the disruptive forces of change. This involves more than just routine interactions or superficial engagements; it calls for a sincere effort to understand the personal and professional aspirations of team members, aligning them with the organization's goals, and ensuring that each member feels valued and understood, an approach that not only enhances team cohesion but also deepens their commitment to the organizational vision.

Moreover, to effectively leverage these relationships for organizational resilience, it is imperative to foster a culture that promotes open communication and regular feedback, enabling a flow of ideas and concerns that can be addressed promptly and effectively. This openness not only helps in preempting potential issues that might arise during times of change but also reinforces the team's role in the collective mission, ensuring that they feel an integral part of the decision-making process and not just passive bystanders. This sense of involvement and ownership is crucial in maintaining high morale and motivation levels, even when the organization is navigating through challenging phases.

Another strategy to strengthen these bonds lies in creating opportunities for team members to connect and collaborate in settings beyond the usual work tasks, such as team-building activities or community service projects, which can provide deeper insights into each other's strengths, weaknesses, and values. These interactions, when guided by the principles of faith and mutual respect, can lead to a more profound understanding and appreciation of each team member's unique contributions to the organization, fostering a sense of unity and shared purpose. This unity becomes a cornerstone on which the resilience of the organization is built, enabling it to not only withstand the pressures of immediate changes but also to emerge stronger and more cohesive in the long run.

Ultimately, the art of leveraging relationships for enhancing organizational resilience is about creating an environment where team members are encouraged to grow, contribute, and thrive even amidst uncertainty. By nurturing these relationships, you are not only safeguarding the organization against the impacts of change but also setting a foundation for sustained growth and success. It is through these strong, resilient relationships that an organization can truly adapt and flourish, reflecting the divine principle that we are stronger together than we are apart, a principle that resonates deeply with every leader who believes in the power of faith and unity.

Recap and Actionable Steps

In reflecting upon the journey through the often tumultuous waves of organizational change, a fundamental realization surfaces, underscoring the essence of navigating through this transformative landscape with a focus on maintaining and enhancing relationships; it becomes clear that as leaders, particularly those who hold their faith and leadership as intertwined threads of their identity, the call to foster resilient, trust-filled relationships is not just a strategic move but a moral imperative. Understanding this, we see that the throes of organizational change provide a unique opportunity not only for personal growth but also for solidifying the bonds that underpin the very fabric of our teams and organizations.

Through the earlier sections of our discussion, we unveiled the complexities and inherent challenges posed by change—be it structural, strategic, or personnel adjustments—and the consequent impact on interpersonal dynamics within an organization. As leaders who seek guidance and wisdom from their faith, acknowledging the inherent value and potential in each relationship is crucial; thus, when an organization undergoes change, it is your responsibility to steer these relationships through uncertain waters with clarity and compassion. The approach to managing these shifts should not merely be reactive but deeply rooted in proactive, strategic foresight that prioritizes open communication and trust.

To actualize the insights and strategies discussed, here are specific, actionable steps that can be directly applied to ensure that relationships within your sphere of influence not only survive but thrive during and after periods of change:

Maintain Open Lines of Communication: Ensure that you regularly update your team on developments within the organization. This could be through weekly briefings or a dedicated communication channel that allows for real-time updates and feedback. Transparency is key—when team members understand the reasons behind changes and their intended outcomes, it cultivates an environment of trust and inclusivity.

Facilitate Regular Feedback Sessions: Organize monthly or bi-weekly meetings where team members can voice their concerns, suggestions, and feelings about ongoing changes. These sessions should be structured to foster openness and honesty, with the assurance that feedback will be received non-judgmentally and considered seriously.

Invest in Relationship-Building Activities: Integrate activities that strengthen bonds and build trust within your team. This could range from team retreats focused on professional development to informal gatherings that allow team members to connect on a personal level. Such activities help in alleviating stress and building camaraderie during times of change.

Provide Support and Resources: Recognize that change can be challenging and, at times, stressful for your team members. Providing access to counseling services or professional development programs can help them manage stress and adapt more effectively to change. Additionally, ensure they have the resources necessary to perform their roles efficiently during transition periods.

Recognize and Reward Resilience: During times of change, acknowledge and reward those who positively embrace and adapt to these changes. Recognition can be as simple as verbal acknowledgment in team meetings or more formal rewards such as certificates or bonuses. This not only boosts morale but also encourages a culture of resilience and adaptability.

Engage in Continuous Learning: As a leader, set an example by continually seeking to improve your own skills in managing change and relationships. Participate in workshops, seminars, or courses on change management and leadership. Applying the knowledge gained to your leadership style will enhance your ability to guide your team effectively through transitions.

Pray for Guidance and Wisdom: In your role as a leader who believes in the power of faith, do not underestimate the strength derived from prayer. Seek divine guidance to lead with empathy and justice in times of uncertainty, and encourage your team to find solace and strength in their faith as well.

By integrating these actionable steps into your leadership approach, you create a robust framework that not only manages but leverages change to forge stronger, more resilient professional relationships. These relationships, built on the foundation of mutual trust and respect, are indispensable assets in the face of inevitable organizational evolutions, serving not only the strategic objectives of the organization but also the collective well-being of all those involved.

In conclusion, as we embrace the challenges and opportunities presented by change, let us remain steadfast in our commitment to nurturing the relationships that are central to our leadership. Let your faith illuminate your path as you guide your team through these transformative times, ensuring that each step taken is grounded in understanding, compassion, and unwavering trust.

The Power of Positivity in Leadership

"For my thoughts are not your thoughts, neither are your ways my ways, saith the LORD. For as the heavens are higher than the earth, so are my ways higher than your ways, and my thoughts than your thoughts." Isaiah 55:8-9

Leaders play a pivotal role in shaping the atmosphere and the performance of their teams. One of the most influential tools a leader has is their mindset. The impact of maintaining a positive mindset is profound, affecting decision-making, team morale, and the overall success of the organization. Understanding and harnessing the power of positivity can transform your leadership and set the foundation for a resilient, thriving team.

The Heart of Positivity in Leadership

At the heart of effective leadership lies the ability to inspire and motivate. This begins with the leader's mindset. A positive mindset isn't just about feeling good; it influences how you see the world, how you confront challenges, and how you interact with others. When a leader chooses to focus on the positive aspects of any situation, they set the stage for constructive responses and innovative solutions.

Consider decision-making. Leaders face decisions every day— some minor, others crucial to the success of their organizations. A positive mindset helps you approach these decisions with a sense of

144

opportunity and potential. It opens your mind, allowing you to see various possibilities and outcomes, rather than becoming bogged down by constraints and limitations. This approach not only leads to better decisions but also instills a sense of confidence and purpose within your team.

Team morale is another area profoundly influenced by a leader's positivity. Teams look to their leaders for cues on how to react to successes and setbacks. If a leader consistently approaches challenges with a positive, can-do attitude, it becomes contagious. Team members are likely to adopt this attitude themselves, leading to enhanced morale and a cooperative team environment. This, in turn, boosts productivity and reduces conflict, creating a workplace where individuals feel valued and inspired to contribute their best.

Now, let's talk about the overall success of an organization. Success in business is not just about having a great product or a solid business plan. It's also about creating an environment where innovation and efficiency thrive. A positive leader acts as a catalyst for this. By fostering a positive atmosphere, they encourage risk-taking within safe boundaries, promote creativity, and facilitate open communication. These elements are crucial for long-term success and can set a company apart from its competitors.

However, positivity on its own is not enough. It becomes truly powerful when coupled with resilience. Challenges and setbacks are inevitable in any leadership journey. Here, the real power of positivity is revealed. A positive attitude helps you view challenges as temporary and surmountable, encouraging a resilient response. It's about bouncing back from setbacks with a renewed focus and minimal downtime.

The relationship between positivity and resilience is symbiotic. While positivity helps in navigating through tough times with hope and determination, resilience allows you to learn and grow from these experiences. This cycle enhances a leader's ability to remain optimistic through future challenges, continuously fostering a resilient and positive team culture.

So, how can you cultivate this powerful combination of positivity and resilience? Start by consciously choosing to focus on the positive in every situation. This doesn't mean ignoring the negatives but rather choosing to give more energy to potential solutions rather than problems. Regularly communicate positive thoughts and affirmations, not only to yourself but also to your team. Acknowledge challenges openly but emphasize the steps you will take to overcome them. Encourage your team to do the same, and celebrate when they approach their work with positivity and resilience.

Moreover, commit to personal and professional growth. Leaders who are learners model the resilience needed to adapt and thrive in changing circumstances. Engage with books, courses, and seminars that not only enhance your skills but also enrich your perspective. This commitment to growth helps in maintaining a positive outlook even in the face of adversity.

Finally, foster a supportive environment where positivity and resilience can flourish. This involves building strong relationships within your team, promoting open communication, and ensuring that everyone feels supported both professionally and personally. When team members feel secure, they are more likely to embrace a positive and resilient mindset, contributing to the ongoing success of the organization.

In conclusion, the power of positivity in leadership is transformative. It influences decision-making, enhances team morale, and contributes to the overall success of an organization. When combined with resilience, it equips leaders and their teams to navigate challenges effectively and emerge stronger. As a leader, nurturing a positive and resilient attitude is not just beneficial; it is essential for sustained success and growth.

Developing Guiding Principles Aligned with Your Values

As a leader, your core values are the foundation upon which you build your behavior and decision-making processes. It is crucial, therefore, to clearly identify what these values are. This process begins with a deep reflection on what is most important to you. What principles guide your life and work? Integrity, accountability, empathy, and innovation are examples of common core values that many leaders uphold. Think about the moments when you felt most fulfilled in your work. What values were you upholding at those times?

Identifying these values clearly is not just about knowing them; it's about living them. To articulate your core values, start by writing down the values that resonate with you. Reflect on each one. Ask yourself why each value matters to you and how it has influenced your past decisions. This reflection helps in making your values concrete, something more than just abstract ideas. Once you have a list, narrow it down to about three to five core values. These should be values you are committed to, no matter the situation.

Translating these values into actionable guiding principles is the next critical step. Guiding principles are like a compass that directs your behavior and decision-making in your leadership journey. They transform your abstract values into practical, day-to-day behaviors and choices. For example, if one of your core values is integrity, a guiding principle could always be to communicate truthfully with your team and stakeholders, even when the news is bad.

Another core value could be innovation. The guiding principle here could be to encourage creativity by allocating time and resources for team members to pursue new ideas. This principle guides your decisions about resource allocation and how you manage your team's time. It makes innovation a practical part of your work week, not just a theoretical ideal.

It is important that these principles are not just written but also communicated clearly to your team. They need to understand not only what the organization's values are but also how these values translate into the everyday operations of the business. This clarity helps in aligning the entire team towards a common goal and manner of conduct, which can significantly enhance teamwork and productivity.

Moreover, guiding principles are not static. As your organization grows and evolves, your understanding of what works best may change. Therefore, revisiting and revising your guiding principles periodically is essential. This ensures they remain relevant and aligned with both your personal values and the needs of your organization. It also helps in adapting to changes in the business environment or in societal norms and expectations.

Establishing and articulating your guiding principles based on your core values is not just a task to be checked off. It is an ongoing commitment to leading by example. By clearly defining and adhering to these principles, you set a standard for others to follow, which can cultivate a strong, values-driven culture within your organization. This culture can become your company's identity, internally and externally, attracting like-minded individuals and creating a cohesive, motivated team.

In summary, as a leader, take time to identify and articulate your core values. Develop guiding principles that translate these values into actionable behaviors. Communicate these principles clearly to your team and integrate them into the everyday operations of your organization. Regularly review and update these principles to ensure they remain relevant. By doing this, you not only enhance your effectiveness as a leader but also contribute positively to the culture and success of your organization.

Practicing Mindfulness and Emotional Regulation

As leaders, the ability to stay composed and in control of our emotions is crucial. This skill impacts our decision-making and how we react under pressure, which in turn influences our entire team. Mindfulness and emotional regulation are tools that can help us achieve this state of control. Let's break these concepts down into simple, actionable steps that you can incorporate into your daily routine.

Mindfulness, in its essence, means being fully present in the moment. It involves being aware of where we are and what we're doing, without being overly reactive to what's going on around us. This can sound easy, but it often requires practice. Mindfulness helps in recognizing our emotional state and allowing us to control our reactions better.

To begin with mindfulness, start by allocating a specific time each day for this practice. Five minutes each morning could be a good starting point. During this time, focus solely on your breathing. Feel the air enter through your nose, filling your lungs, and then slowly exhale through your mouth. This practice helps in centering your thoughts and clearing your mind of distractions.

Beyond just breathing exercises, mindfulness can be practiced throughout the day. For instance, while eating, pay attention to the taste, texture, and aroma of your food. When walking, notice the sensations in your feet as they touch the ground. This continuous practice of awareness brings you back to the present moment, helping you keep a clear mind.

Emotional regulation, on the other hand, involves understanding, managing, and responding to your emotions in a way that is considered, constructive, and in alignment with your values. It's about not letting your emotions get the better of you, but rather using them to make informed decisions.

A simple technique to improve emotional regulation is the 'stop, breathe, reflect, choose' method. When a situation arises that triggers a strong emotional response, first stop. Do not react immediately. Next, take a deep breath to give yourself a moment to calm down. Reflect then on why you are feeling this emotion and what it might be signalling. Finally, choose how to respond in a way that aligns with your goals and values.

Journaling is another effective tool for emotional regulation. At the end of each day, take a few minutes to write down the emotions you felt throughout the day and the situations that triggered them. This practice can help you identify patterns in your emotional responses and increase your self-awareness, making it easier to manage similar situations in the future.

Mindfulness and emotional regulation are deeply interconnected. Mindfulness provides the awareness necessary to recognize our emotions, and emotional regulation gives us the tools to manage and respond to these emotions appropriately. Together, they empower us to lead with a clear and composed mind.

Implementing these techniques may not only improve your leadership skills but can also reduce stress, enhance focus, and increase empathy towards others. This makes you not just a better leader, but also a positive influence on your team, promoting a healthier, more productive work environment.

To make these practices part of your routine, start small. Choose one mindfulness exercise and one emotional regulation technique to practice daily. As these skills become a natural part of your day, you'll find your ability to handle leadership challenges with greater ease improving significantly.

Remember, the goal of integrating mindfulness and emotional regulation into your leadership practice is not to suppress your emotions but to understand and channel them in productive ways. Over time, these practices will enhance your ability to lead with resilience and adaptability, qualities that define great leaders.

Adopting mindfulness and emotional regulation can transform your leadership style and possibly your life, leading to decisions that are balanced, considered, and empathetic. Let these tools help you navigate the complexities of leadership with grace and effectiveness.

Building a Support System for Resilience

Leaders often face numerous challenges. It is essential to have a support system. This system consists of people you trust. They offer support and encourage you when you face challenges.

Why is this important? A strong support network provides advice, encouragement, and a fresh perspective. These can be crucial during tough times. When a leader faces difficult decisions or setbacks, knowing there are trusted individuals to turn to can make a significant difference.

Let's explore how you can build and maintain a support system. This system will help you remain resilient and effective in your leadership role.

First, identify potential members of your support system. These should be individuals you trust deeply. They could be peers, mentors, family members, or close friends. The key is to choose people who understand your values and goals. They should be individuals who can provide honest feedback and encouragement.

Once you have identified these individuals, reach out to them. Explain why you value their perspective and would appreciate their support. This can be done through a personal meeting, a phone call, or a heartfelt letter. Expressing your appreciation for their role in your life helps to strengthen these bonds.

Next, establish regular communication. This could be scheduled meetings or informal check-ins. The frequency of these interactions will depend on your needs and the nature of your relationship with each support member. Consistent communication helps to build trust and ensures that your supporters are updated on your challenges and successes.

It is also essential to be there for your support network. Support is a two-way street. Offer your encouragement and help to your supporters. This reciprocal relationship not only strengthens bonds but also enriches your leadership qualities.

In addition to personal connections, professional networks can also serve as part of your support system. Joining leadership groups, professional associations, or online communities can provide you with access to a broader range of perspectives and advice. These platforms allow you to connect with other leaders facing similar challenges. They can be invaluable resources for support and inspiration.

Maintaining your support system is as important as building it. Keep your interactions genuine and respectful. Show appreciation for the support you receive. Be proactive in addressing any issues that might affect your relationships. A healthy support system requires ongoing attention and care.

Finally, remember that the purpose of your support system is to help you maintain resilience in your leadership role. This system is not just for times of crisis but also for sharing successes. Celebrate your achievements with your support network. This not only fosters a positive environment but also motivates you and your supporters to continue striving for excellence.

In summary, a support system is crucial for any leader. It provides emotional and practical support, which is essential for overcoming challenges and achieving goals. By carefully building and maintaining your support network, you ensure that you have the resilience needed to succeed as a leader. Take the steps today to establish this vital component of effective leadership. Your future self will thank you for the support and strength it provides.

Celebrating Achievements and Maintaining Motivation

In leadership and life, noticing and acknowledging your achievements is vital. It's not just about giving yourself a pat on the back. It's about recognizing the hard work that you and your team put in. This recognition fuels further effort and enthusiasm. When a leader celebrates these wins, big or small, it sets a positive tone in the team. It shows that progress is valued just as much as the end result.

Why is celebrating achievements important? First, it helps to build a culture of appreciation and success within your team or organization. When team members see that their efforts are recognized, they feel valued. This feeling of being valued boosts morale and increases their commitment to their work. As a leader, your acknowledgment can transform the regular workflow into a more dynamic and motivated environment.

How do you effectively celebrate these achievements? Start with setting clear goals and milestones. These should be specific, measurable, attainable, relevant, and time-bound—what many know as SMART criteria. When these goals are met, acknowledge them. This could be through a simple team meeting where you highlight the achievement, a thank-you note, or something more public like a mention in a company newsletter or a social media post.

It's also essential to personalize your recognition. Different people may appreciate different types of acknowledgment. Some might prefer public recognition, while others might value a private thank-you. Getting to know what makes your team members feel valued is a part of your job as a leader.

While celebrating achievements, it's equally important to maintain motivation, especially after reaching a significant milestone or at the completion of a project. It's common for teams to experience a dip in motivation after a big achievement. This is often called the "post-success slump." To counter this, you need to set new goals promptly. This doesn't mean rushing into new projects without a break, but rather gradually setting the stage for the next challenges.

Maintaining motivation can be nurtured by fostering a growth mindset within your team. This involves encouraging continuous learning and development. Provide opportunities for your team members to upgrade their skills or learn new ones. Encourage them to set personal development goals that align with their roles and the organization's objectives.

Another technique is to keep the communication lines open. Ask for feedback about what they need to stay motivated. Do they need more challenges? More support? More flexibility? Listening and responding to your team's needs shows that you value their input and are committed to their growth and satisfaction.

Motivation can also be maintained by ensuring that the work environment is positive and supportive. This includes everything from the physical space to the emotional climate. Ensure your team has the tools and resources they need to perform their jobs effectively. This removes unnecessary stress and barriers that could dampen motivation.

Finally, always link back to the bigger picture. It's important for team members to understand how their work fits into the organization's goals. This understanding helps them see the value of their contributions and motivates them to keep pushing forward.

In conclusion, celebrating achievements and maintaining motivation are crucial for sustained success in any leadership role. By recognizing hard work and continuously fostering a supportive and growth-oriented environment, you can ensure that your team remains engaged and productive. Remember, a motivated team is a successful team.

Actionable Steps for Cultivating a Positive and Resilient Attitude

As a leader, cultivating a positive and resilient attitude is essential. This chapter focuses on practical steps you can take to develop these crucial traits. Each action outlined here is designed to help you integrate positivity and resilience into your daily leadership practice.

The first actionable step involves identifying your top three core values. Core values are the fundamental beliefs that guide your actions, decisions, and interactions with others. It is important for you as a leader to clearly understand what these are as they shape every aspect of your leadership style.

To start, take a piece of paper and write down all the values that resonate with you. These could include integrity, courage, innovation, respect, or service. Once you have a list, prioritize them based on what truly drives your actions and decisions the most. Select the top three that feel most critical to your identity and work. This process not only helps clarify your principles but also ensures that your leadership actions are aligned with these values.

The next step is to develop a set of guiding principles that align with your top three values. Guiding principles are like a roadmap for how to act in various situations. For example, if one of your core values is respect, a guiding principle might be to always listen actively and empathetically to team members. To create these, consider the following:

- What actions can you take daily to reflect this value?
- How can these values guide your decision-making processes?
- What behaviors should you avoid to stay true to these values?

Write down specific guiding principles for each value and commit to following them in your daily leadership practice.

The third step is to practice one mindfulness technique daily to strengthen your mental resilience and focus. Mindfulness involves being fully present and engaged in the moment without distraction or judgment. A simple technique to start with is deep breathing, which can help reduce stress and improve concentration.

Each day, spend five minutes in a quiet space practicing deep breathing. Concentrate on your breath, inhaling slowly through your nose and exhaling through your mouth. Try to clear your mind of other thoughts and focus solely on your breathing. This practice can serve as a powerful tool to calm your mind before making important decisions or during stressful situations.

Another actionable step is to reach out to a trusted friend or colleague each week. The goal here is to build and maintain a support network, which is vital for resilience. During these interactions, express gratitude for their support and offer your support in return. This could be through a quick call, an email, or a coffee meeting.

Showing appreciation can strengthen your relationships and increase your circle of support, while offering help reinforces your role as a leader who cares about the growth and well-being of others.

Finally, dedicate time each week to reflect on and celebrate your achievements and those of your team. This practice not only boosts morale but also encourages a positive outlook among your team members. Recognizing accomplishments, no matter how small, reinforces the behavior you want to see in your team and boosts collective resilience to face future challenges.

Here's how you can implement this:

- Set aside an hour each week to review what you and your team have accomplished.

- Make a list of these achievements and discuss them at your team meetings.

- Encourage your team members to share their successes and learnings.

- Celebrate these achievements formally, such as through awards, acknowledgments in newsletters, or even casual mentions in meetings.

By taking these steps, you as a leader will not only foster a more positive and resilient attitude in yourself but also set a powerful example for your team. Remember, leadership is not just about directing others but also about setting a standard of behavior and attitude that others aspire to emulate. Implementing these practices will help you become a leader who inspires positivity and resilience, driving your team toward greater success.

Proactivity in Leadership

"How precious to me are your thoughts,[a] God!

How vast is the sum of them! Were I to count them,

they would outnumber the grains of sand—

when I awake, I am still with you." Psalms 139:17-18

Problems and Context

As leaders who uphold our faith and values, it is crucial to understand the importance of being proactive in our leadership roles, as this approach not only fosters a positive atmosphere but also cascades down to enhance overall team morale and organizational success; when we talk about being proactive, we are referring to the ability to anticipate future challenges and initiate appropriate responses rather than simply reacting to events after they occur, which can often lead to hurried decisions that may not align with our best practices or the values we cherish. The proactive approach is deeply embedded in the idea of foresight and planning, allowing leaders to create strategies that align closely with their organization's objectives and ethical guidelines, thus, ensuring that every step taken is a reflection of calculated, thoughtful decision-making processes that consider not only the immediate benefits but also the long-term impacts on the organization's health and its people.

162

Understanding that environments, especially in leadership roles, can often become fast-paced and demanding, maintaining a proactive stance can, indeed, present challenges; these challenges primarily revolve around the constant need to be ahead in thinking and decision-making, which requires a continuous feed of information and an acute awareness of the ever-changing dynamics within and outside the organization. However, the benefits of maintaining such proactivity are immense, not only does it prevent the organization from undergoing possible negative consequences of reactive decisions, such as rushed, less informed decisions that could lead to conflicts or missed opportunities, but it also sets a strong example for all team members, encouraging them to adopt similar behaviors that contribute positively to their work and personal growth.

Conversely, the consequences of adhering solely to a reactive leadership style can significantly affect the long-term health of an organization; when leaders constantly react to situations without preemptive measures, it often leads to a culture of short-sightedness and quick fixes, this not only hampers the development of a robust organizational strategy but may also lead to decreased morale among team members who might feel that their work environment is unstable or unpredictably dictated by external pressures. It is, therefore, essential to cultivate a proactive mindset, which involves regularly evaluating potential future scenarios and equipping oneself and the team with the tools and knowledge to handle forthcoming challenges efficiently and in alignment with the core beliefs and objectives of the organization.

The impact of a proactive leadership style extends beyond just organizational success; it positively influences team morale, as team members feel more secure and supported in a work environment where leaders demonstrate foresight and a clear direction. This sense of security comes from knowing that their leaders are not merely reacting to problems as they arise but are actively working to foresee and mitigate potential issues, which speaks volumes about the leader's commitment to the organization and its people, thereby fostering a strong, trust-based relationship between leaders and their teams. Such environments encourage open communication, innovation, and a willingness among team members to contribute proactively to the organization's goals, knowing well that their efforts align with a well-thought-out plan that considers their welfare and professional growth.

In conclusion, embracing proactivity in leadership is not just about staying one step ahead in strategy and operations; it is about nurturing an organizational culture that values foresight, preparedness, and ethical decision-making, aligning these values with the core religious beliefs that guide us as leaders in our daily actions and interactions. By choosing to be proactive, leaders can ensure that their organizations do not just survive but thrive in competitive and complex environments, reflecting the strength and stability of their foundational values and beliefs.

Understanding Proactivity in Leadership

When we talk about being a proactive leader, we are referring to the type of leader who does not simply react to situations as they arise, but rather, one who plans ahead, anticipates challenges, and takes decisive actions to avoid or mitigate potential issues before they can have a significant impact on their team or organization; this is fundamentally what sets apart proactive leadership from reactive leadership, which tends to deal with problems only after they have occurred, often leading to rushed decisions and increased stress among team members.

The differences between proactive and reactive leadership styles are stark and significant, illustrating two fundamentally different approaches to managing and leading within an organization; proactive leaders tend to engage in thorough planning and foresee possible future scenarios, which allows them to handle challenges more smoothly and efficiently, whereas reactive leaders often find themselves in a perpetual state of catch-up, which can lead to decision fatigue and a reactive loop where problems continue to arise because they were not adequately addressed the first time.

The role of foresight and planning in proactive leadership cannot be overstated because it is the cornerstone of effective leadership and strategic management; by consistently looking ahead and anticipating the needs of the organization, proactive leaders can develop strategies and implement systems that address these needs before they become urgent, which not only helps in maintaining a calm, controlled work environment but also in fostering a culture where team members feel prepared and supported in their roles.

Proactivity influences decision-making and problem-solving in several profound ways; first, it allows leaders to gather information, weigh options, and consult with key stakeholders before making decisions, which often leads to more thoughtful, informed, and effective outcomes, second, proactive problem-solving means that potential issues are identified and addressed before they escalate, which saves time and resources and prevents the kind of crises that can derail organizational progress and morale.

In embracing the principles of proactive leadership, every leader who believes in the guiding hand of divine wisdom can see the reflection of their faith in their work by trusting that their foresight and diligent planning are in themselves acts of faith, aligning their actions with the belief that they are guided not only by their skills and knowledge but also by the greater good they aim to serve, ultimately making them not just leaders in their fields but also stewards of the values they hold dear.

Thus, understanding and implementing proactive leadership is not only about enhancing organizational effectiveness but also about embodying the values that define good, ethical leadership, connecting the dots between daily management tasks and larger, spiritual ambitions; this holistic approach to leadership not only ensures better outcomes for the organization but also enriches the personal and spiritual lives of the leaders themselves, creating a loop of positive reinforcement that promotes overall growth and satisfaction.

Developing Proactive Behaviors

When you, as a leader who holds faith close, start to think about being more proactive in your leadership, it's like preparing to plant a garden that you wish to see flourish; you must understand the tools and seeds you need, prepare the soil, and commit to the nurturing process daily. Developing proactive behaviors in both your personal and professional life is foundational to this process, involving a shift in mindset from merely reacting to circumstances as they arise, to anticipating and preparing for them ahead of time. This proactive approach not only prepares you to handle challenges more effectively but also positions you to lead with confidence and foresight, embodying the wisdom that often comes from the teachings you cherish.

One effective strategy to cultivate this proactive mindset begins with setting aside time each day for reflection and planning. This is not just about glancing at your calendar and to-do list but deeply analyzing potential future scenarios and developing action plans. This practice might seem time-consuming at first, but like prayer or meditation, it becomes a crucial part of your day, offering a framework through which you can view potential challenges and opportunities from a place of preparedness rather than panic. Encouraging this kind of thinking in your team can also transform the dynamics of your group, setting a standard for thoughtful anticipation of needs and strategic responses.

Beyond individual reflection, adopting techniques to anticipate challenges is fundamental to proactive leadership. Scenario planning, for instance, is a tool you can use to forecast future scenarios based on current trends within your industry or the world at large. This method involves identifying key variables that impact your organization and imagining various ways they might evolve. This process should be detailed and thorough, considering both best-case and worst-case scenarios, thereby equipping you with strategies to handle diverse outcomes. Engaging your team in this activity not only prepares them to think ahead but also fosters a culture of resilience and adaptability.

Transitioning from a reactive to a proactive decision-making model in your leadership style is a monumental shift that requires deliberate actions and decisions. This transition can begin with small, daily decisions that focus on long-term benefits rather than immediate relief or results. Over time, this incremental approach can significantly alter your decision-making process, aligning more with a proactive framework. Moreover, this shift also involves recognizing the triggers that often push you toward reactive decisions—such as pressure from peers or an overpacked schedule—and intentionally creating buffers to mitigate these influences.

Furthermore, tools for scenario planning and risk assessment are indispensable in the toolkit of a proactive leader. These tools help you visualize the potential impact of various decisions and plan for unforeseen events. Software and methodologies are available that can guide you through this process, providing structured ways to evaluate risks associated with different scenarios. This kind of preparation not only aids in making informed decisions but also in communicating these decisions to your team or board, providing clear rationales backed by thorough analysis.

Finally, fostering proactive thinking within your team can be achieved through regular training sessions focused on strategic thinking and problem-solving. These sessions can be structured around real-world problems or hypothetical situations relevant to your industry. The goal is to challenge team members to think ahead, assess possible outcomes, and develop strategic responses. This not only enhances their ability to think proactively but also reinforces a team culture where foresight is valued and cultivated.

In conclusion, developing proactive behaviors involves a comprehensive approach that integrates personal development, strategic planning, and team engagement. By adopting these strategies, you can transform not only your approach to leadership but also instill a proactive mindset within your organization, leading to more thoughtful, foresighted, and resilient leadership. Remember, the journey to proactive leadership is continuous and requires commitment and patience, much like nurturing a garden, but the results—thriving teams and successful outcomes—are well worth the effort.

Overcoming Barriers to Proactivity

In every journey of leadership, especially for those who hold their faith as a guide, encountering barriers when trying to be proactive rather than reactive is as inevitable as the sunrise, yet, understanding these common hurdles can transform your challenges into stepping stones toward greater effectiveness and alignment with God's purpose for your role. One widespread barrier is the existing organizational culture which might resist change or new proactive approaches because it is often easier to continue with the known rather than to venture into the unknown, which requires new strategies and sometimes, a shift in values or routines that have been long established.

To methodically address this issue, it is crucial to first establish a clear vision of what proactivity looks like specifically for your context—this vision should not only align with the organizational goals but also resonate deeply with your personal faith and how you perceive your leadership role under God's guidance. Once this vision is clear, articulate it consistently and passionately to your teams, ensuring it permeates every level of the organization through regular communication, be it meetings, newsletters, or informal talks. This constant reinforcement helps in gradually shifting the culture, making the soil fertile for proactive initiatives to take root.

Another significant barrier is time management, which often seems like a relentless flood, sweeping away all the neatly arranged plans for proactive strategies. To navigate this, one effective technique is to prioritize tasks not just by urgency but by their importance in achieving the proactive vision you have set. This might mean scheduling strategic planning sessions well in advance and guarding that time zealously, which demonstrates to others the value you place on proactivity. It also might involve delegating reactive tasks where possible, empowering your team members to handle day-to-day crises, which frees up your capacity to focus on forward-thinking tasks.

Fear of failure is another towering barrier that can paralyze even the most experienced leaders; this fear is particularly potent because it strikes directly at our insecurities and can make us question our path and decisions. As a leader in faith, it is helpful to remember that every failure is a step towards growth and understanding God's plan more deeply. Encourage yourself and your team to view failures as learning opportunities and to embrace calculated risks. This does not mean being reckless but rather, having the courage to step out with the best planning and preparation, knowing that regardless of the outcome, there will be valuable insights gained.

Finally, promoting calculated risk-taking involves creating an environment where such risks are supported and learned from. This requires setting up a system where risks are assessed, discussed openly, and managed effectively. It also means celebrating those moments when taking a calculated risk leads to a breakthrough, thus reinforcing the value of stepping out of comfort zones. By consistently applying these strategies, you not only overcome barriers to proactivity but also enhance your capacity to lead effectively, guided by your faith and commitment to God's calling for you as a leader.

Measuring the Impact of Proactivity

In the journey of leadership, especially for those who hold their faith dear, the concept of proactivity is not merely about taking early actions but aligns closely with stewardship and foresight, virtues highly regarded in both spiritual and managerial realms. When a leader decides to embrace proactivity, they are not just choosing to be ahead in problems and solutions, but also aligning their actions with the divine principle of preparedness, which is both a responsibility and a form of worship. Therefore, understanding how to measure the impact of such proactivity becomes crucial, not just for the health of the organization but for the moral and ethical alignment of the leader's actions with their faith. Tools and metrics, when rightly utilized, serve as the compass that guides this alignment, ensuring that each step taken is not only forward but also upward in terms of moral and ethical standards.

Introducing the right tools to assess the effectiveness of proactive leadership starts with identifying what metrics are relevant to your organization's goals and your personal leadership values, which is an exploration that requires both time and patience. One must look into both quantitative measures, such as increase in productivity, and qualitative measures, such as improved team morale or enhanced stakeholder satisfaction. It is imperative to have a balanced approach toward both these metrics, as focusing solely on numbers might lead to a mechanical view of progress, whereas just concentrating on qualitative aspects might not provide the clear markers needed for strategic planning and assessment. This balance ensures that the leadership remains dynamic and responsive to both human and business needs, which in turn fosters a culture of growth and accountability.

Incorporating feedback mechanisms is another foundational step in measuring proactivity; however, feedback must be sought not only from peers and subordinates but also from oneself, through regular self-assessment and reflection guided by one's values and spiritual insights. This dual feedback mechanism ensures that the leadership is not only approved by others but also by one's own conscience, which is critical for leaders who believe in moral and spiritual accountability. Regular intervals of reflection and feedback help in creating a loop of continuous improvement, where each cycle of feedback is an opportunity to align closer with both organizational goals and personal ethical standards, thereby making the leadership journey not only about leading others but also about self-mastery and personal growth.

Quantifying the benefits of proactive leadership on organizational performance might initially seem like a task inclined more towards material gains, but when viewed through the lens of stewardship, it transforms into an act of measuring the efficacy of one's service to their community and workplace. By setting benchmarks for what successful proactivity looks like, whether it's reducing turnaround times for projects, decreasing employee turnover, or increasing customer satisfaction, leaders can have tangible evidence of their service's impact. These benchmarks provide not only a goal to strive for but also a clear metric for spiritual and ethical reflection, transforming each goal achieved into a testament of faithful stewardship.

Lastly, integrating these proactivity metrics into leadership evaluation processes is not just about incorporating them into annual performance reviews but making them a part of the daily leadership practice. When metrics become a daily reference, they cease to be mere numbers and transform into constant reminders of the leader's commitment to their faith, their team, and their mission. The regular interaction with these metrics cultivates an environment where every decision is made with a proactive mindset, and every action is evaluated against the highest standards of faith-based ethical leadership. Thus, the process of integration not only measures but also enhances the quality of leadership, making it a living example of proactive and principled governance.

In conclusion, measuring the impact of proactivity in leadership, especially for leaders who integrate their faith into their professional practices, is about much more than business metrics; it's about creating a system of continual ethical evaluation that aligns every business achievement with spiritual growth and moral responsibility. Through the careful selection and application of appropriate tools and metrics, leaders can transform their everyday responsibilities into opportunities for spiritual and communal service, thereby fulfilling their dual role as both leaders and faithful stewards.

Recap and Actionable Steps

After exploring the significance and the nuts and bolts of proactive leadership, it becomes clear that embracing a proactive approach isn't just beneficial; it's a crucial element for any leader who aspires to lead effectively, especially those who hold their faith in God and see their leadership role as a service to others. Being proactive means not only anticipating what might come but also preparing yourself and your team to handle challenges in a way that aligns with the values you cherish, including those derived from your faith.

Let's delve into a summary of what makes proactive leadership so vital. A proactive leader does not wait for situations to deteriorate; instead, they anticipate potential issues and execute plans to address them before they escalate. This forward-thinking approach not only prevents many crises but also promotes a sense of security and trust within the team, showing that you, as a leader, are committed to the well-being of your projects and your people. Now, reflecting on these insights, we identify that your role as a leader involves being a beacon of hope and reliability, mirroring the steadfastness that faith often teaches.

Here is a step-by-step guide on how you can foster and maintain proactivity in your leadership practices:

Start with Self-Reflection: Daily, take a moment to reflect on your day. Ask yourself what went well and what could have been handled differently. This practice will fine-tune your ability to anticipate and plan, making you a more proactive leader.

Engage in Continuous Learning: Commit to learning something new about your field, your team, or leadership in general each week. This could be through books, workshops, or discussions with fellow leaders. Continuous learning fuels your ability to foresee changes and adapt strategies accordingly.

Implement a Morning Planning Session: Spend the first 15 minutes of your day planning your tasks and anticipating potential challenges. This not only sets a productive tone for the day but also helps you stay ahead of potential issues.

Encourage Team Feedback: Regularly ask for feedback from your team about processes and decisions. This practice not only helps in making more informed decisions but also cultivates a proactive culture within your team as they feel their input is valued and acted upon.

Develop a Risk Management Plan: Work with your team to identify potential risks in your projects or in the day-to-day operations of your team. Develop strategies to mitigate these risks before they become issues. This might include regular training sessions for team members or setting up contingency funds for unexpected financial needs.

Practice Scenario Planning: Regularly engage in scenario planning exercises with your team. These sessions should cover best-case, normal, and worst-case scenarios, helping everyone to think ahead and prepare for various possibilities, reinforcing a proactive mindset.

As you cultivate these habits, remember that your leadership is not just about guiding others but about stewarding the resources and responsibilities you have been entrusted with, much like the stewardship principles taught in many faiths. These practices not only make you a more effective leader but also resonate deeply with your role as a faith-based leader, where foresight and stewardship play significant roles.

In conclusion, stepping up as a proactive leader not only enhances your capability to manage your team effectively but also aligns closely with the ethical and moral standards that guide your life. This alignment brings not only success in your professional endeavors but also fulfills a deeper sense of purpose in your role as a leader. By following these actionable steps, you are not just preparing for a more successful career but also nurturing a legacy that reflects the values you hold dear.

Embrace these steps, integrate them into your daily routine, and watch as your leadership transforms not only your life but also the lives of those you lead. Your journey as a proactive, faith-driven leader is not only about anticipating the future but creating it in a way that aligns with your deepest beliefs and values.

Synthesizing Leadership Insights: A Comprehensive Review

A Deep Dive into Leadership Themes and Strategies

Throughout this book, we've journeyed together through varied terrains of leadership, encountering numerous challenges and strategies that leaders face in today's dynamic environments; now, it's time to pull all these threads together into a cohesive tapestry that can give you a firm foundation when you face your leadership challenges. By revisiting each pivotal theme and strategy discussed, we aim to reinforce your understanding and equip you with a robust toolset that is not only theoretical but highly practical and applicable in your daily leadership roles. It's essential to acknowledge how these concepts are not standalone ideas but rather interconnected elements that, when combined, form a potent formula for effective leadership. This synthesis is not just a recap—it's a consolidation of knowledge aimed at strengthening your capability to navigate through tough periods with confidence and agility.

Leadership isn't just about making decisions or directing teams; it's about understanding the subtle interplays between different leadership styles, the nuances of communication, and the importance of emotional intelligence in fostering an environment where everyone feels valued and motivated. Each chapter of this book has contributed a building block to understanding these complex dynamics, emphasizing the necessity of a holistic approach where strategy, empathy, and adaptability converge to create not just a good leader, but a great one. Reflecting on these chapters allows us to appreciate the full spectrum of leadership qualities and how they can be tailored to meet specific challenges in a rapidly evolving world.

The journey of leadership growth is akin to navigating a ship through stormy seas—the captain must be aware of all the instruments at their disposal, understand the temperaments of their crew, and be prepared for unforeseen obstacles. Similarly, this book has equipped you with the instruments of knowledge, understanding of human behaviors within teams, and strategies to overcome obstacles. By revisiting these insights, we can ensure that no detail, no matter how small, is overlooked in your growth as a leader. This thorough review serves as your compass, helping you to steer your leadership journey with precision and foresight.

Reflections on Leadership Growth

As we reflect on the journey this book has taken you through, it's important to recognize your own growth as a reader and a leader. From the initial understanding of basic leadership principles to the complex strategies for managing change and conflict, your arsenal of skills has expanded significantly. Reflection is a powerful tool in leadership; it allows us to see not only where we've been but also to gauge where we are heading. This book's journey has hopefully shown you that growth is not just about acquiring new skills but also about deepening your understanding of the principles that drive effective leadership. By seeing how various chapters interlink and build upon each other, you can appreciate the layered nature of leadership and the depth of insight required to lead successfully under various circumstances.

Leadership growth is not a destination but a continuous journey of learning and adaptation. As you move forward, remember the insights shared throughout the book, but also remain open to new ideas and perspectives that may challenge your current thinking. The true hallmark of a great leader is the ability to adapt and grow from these challenges, never settling but always striving to improve. This book is a stepping stone in your leadership path, and as you continue to build on these foundations, your potential to lead effectively through tough periods will only increase.

In conclusion, synthesizing the insights gained from this book is more than just an academic exercise; it is a practical endeavor that aims to arm you with the knowledge, skills, and perspectives necessary to navigate the complexities of modern leadership. By taking these lessons to heart and applying them conscientiously in your leadership practice, you are setting the stage for not only personal success but also for the success of your teams and your organization as a whole. Remember, effective leadership is about making a positive impact on the lives of those you lead, and with the comprehensive review of the strategies and themes discussed, you are well on your way to achieving just that.

The Power of Transformative Leadership: Encouragement and Vision

As we draw near the conclusion of this journey through the exploration of leadership, it becomes imperative for us to pause and reflect upon the immense power that transformative leadership holds, not just within the confines of organizational walls, but extending far beyond, into personal growth and community influence. Transformative leaders are not born overnight; they are sculpted through persistent effort, continuous learning, and an unwavering commitment to bettering themselves and the people around them. This type of leadership transcends traditional management tactics, focusing instead on inspiring change and encouraging growth in every encounter and decision.

Imagine you are at a point where the skills and insights you've gained are not just concepts in a book, but tools in your hands, ready to be used to craft a better environment for yourself and your team. The benefits of enhancing your leadership skills are multifaceted, affecting various aspects of both personal and professional life. By embracing the strategies discussed throughout this book, you can elevate your leadership capabilities, which in turn will enhance team productivity, improve interpersonal relationships, and foster a positive organizational culture that thrives on mutual respect and collaborative success. This improvement in the organizational atmosphere is a direct result of effective, thoughtful leadership.

Moreover, the impact of implementing these leadership strategies is vast, creating ripples that extend into all corners of your life and work. As a leader, your actions and decisions set the tone for your team's approach to challenges and opportunities alike. With the right leadership approach, you can transform challenges into stepping stones for success and turn everyday opportunities into exceptional breakthroughs that push your team toward unprecedented heights. The potential for significant positive change is enormous, and it all starts with the decision to apply the insights and techniques you have learned.

However, the journey of leadership does not end here; it is an ongoing path of evolution and growth. True leaders recognize that their development is never complete. They are committed to continuous learning and adaptation, striving always to be better than they were yesterday. This commitment to personal and professional growth is what sets transformative leaders apart. It's about not settling for good enough but pushing the boundaries of what is possible through constant learning and adapting.

Thus, I encourage you, as a reader and a leader, to view this book not just as a source of advice but as a starting point for a deeper, more comprehensive journey into the world of transformative leadership. Embrace the principles laid out in these pages, apply them diligently, and continue to seek out new knowledge and experiences. By doing so, you will not only enhance your own capabilities but also inspire those around you to strive for greater heights. Your journey as a transformative leader is just beginning, and the path ahead is filled with opportunities for growth, impact, and fulfillment.

From Theory to Practice: A Comprehensive Action Plan

When you've been pouring over strategies and leadership theories, it often feels like standing at the edge of a vast ocean, knowing you need to cross it but without a clear path forward; this is where our comprehensive action plan comes into play, designed meticulously to bridge the gap between theoretical knowledge and practical application, ensuring that every leader, regardless of their experience or the challenges they face, can navigate these waters with confidence and a clear sense of direction. This action plan is not just a list of tasks; it's a strategic guide, meticulously crafted to ensure you can implement the lessons learned throughout this book into your daily leadership practices, starting with a detailed step-by-step guide that summarizes the actionable takeaways from each chapter, ensuring that you have a clear and concise reference that you can turn to at any time.

As leaders, when faced with tough times, the temptation is often to revert to what feels comfortable or to make rapid decisions under pressure; however, the first step in our action plan involves a reflective practice that asks you to pause and consider the various strategies discussed, integrating them slowly and thoughtfully into your decision-making process, thereby allowing you to make informed, strategic choices that are not just reactions to immediate pressures but are aligned with long-term goals. This reflective practice is complemented by practical exercises that aim to reinforce your learning and deepen your understanding of each principle discussed; these are not merely theoretical exercises, but hands-on practical tasks that you can incorporate into your daily routine, ensuring that the transition from theory to practice is smooth and effective.

Furthermore, the inclusion of timeline suggestions for implementing various aspects of these leadership principles is crucial, as it provides a structured timeline which helps in pacing the changes you wish to implement, ensuring that each step is manageable and measurable; this gradual implementation helps in mitigating the overwhelming feeling that often accompanies significant changes, enabling you to focus on one aspect at a time, thus maximizing the effectiveness of each strategy implemented. These timeline suggestions are designed to be flexible, allowing you to adjust them based on your specific circumstances and the unique challenges that your organization might be facing, thereby providing a customized approach that is sensitive to your needs and those of your organization.

To further aid in this transition from theory to practice, our action plan also includes practical reflections at the end of each week;

these are designed to help you assess the progress you've made, reflect on the challenges encountered, and adjust your approach accordingly. This continual process of reflection ensures that the strategies you implement are not static but are constantly evolving in response to the changing dynamics of your leadership environment, thus ensuring that they remain relevant and effective. This dynamic approach to implementation not only enhances the adaptability of the strategies discussed but also encourages a culture of continuous learning and adaptation within your team, fostering an environment where growth and development are actively pursued.

In conclusion, as you navigate through the complexities of leadership, especially during challenging times, remember that the transition from theory to practice is not an event but a journey. It requires patience, persistence, and a willingness to adapt and learn. By following this comprehensive action plan, you are not just applying theories but are actively engaging in a process of transformation, one that promises not only to enhance your skills as a leader but also to empower those around you, creating a ripple effect of positive change throughout your organization. As you embark on this journey, keep in mind that each step you take is a building block in the construction of a robust leadership style that is not only effective but also resilient, capable of withstanding the pressures of any tough period and emerging stronger on the other side.

The Journey Continues: A Call to Transformative Leadership

As you reach the end of this book, it's critical to understand that the journey of enhancing your leadership capabilities does not conclude with the final pages of this text; rather, it marks the beginning of an ongoing process of growth, learning, and application of the principles you have encountered throughout this reading, and this chapter is dedicated to empowering you to take proactive steps towards becoming a transformative leader. The path to transformative leadership is not a quick sprint but a marathon that requires persistence, continuous learning, and the consistent application of the strategies you have learned. Engaging with supplementary resources and training programs is not just an option; it's a necessary step for those who are serious about making substantial improvements in their leadership style and effectiveness.

Let us delve deeper into the significance of continuous learning for a leader, especially during tough periods, where challenges and uncertainties can make it easy to fall back on old habits that may not serve the best interest of your team or organization. Continuous learning involves actively seeking out new knowledge, skills, and experiences that can help you respond more effectively to emerging challenges. It requires a commitment to stepping out of your comfort zone and embracing the discomfort that often accompanies growth. To support

187

your journey, consider engaging with books, online courses, webinars, and workshops that focus on areas of leadership that you find most challenging or where you see the greatest opportunity for growth.

In addition to self-guided learning, participating in formal training programs can provide structured learning experiences that help reinforce the concepts covered in this book. These programs often offer the added benefit of connecting you with other leaders who can share their experiences, challenges, and solutions, thereby expanding your perspective and enhancing your problem-solving skills. Now, let's consider the role of supplementary resources; these are invaluable in providing ongoing support and deep dives into specific areas of leadership. For instance, subscribing to leadership podcasts, following thought leaders on social media, and joining leadership forums online can keep you updated on the latest developments in the field and introduce you to innovative ideas and strategies that you can tailor to your own leadership context.

The commitment to specific leadership improvements is also vital to your growth as a leader. This involves setting clear, actionable goals based on the insights you have gained from this book. For example, if you have identified effective communication as an area for improvement, you might set a goal to implement regular feedback sessions with your team, utilizing the techniques discussed in the chapters on communication and team management. By setting specific goals and tracking your progress, you reinforce the application of new skills and ensure that your learning translates into tangible improvements in your leadership effectiveness.

Finally, let's talk about the inspiration to become agents of positive change in your organizations and communities. Transformative leadership is not just about improving your own skills and advancing your career; it's about making a meaningful impact on the people around you and contributing to the success of your organization. By embodying the principles of transformative leadership, you inspire others to also embrace these practices, creating a culture of continuous improvement and innovation. This chapter is a call to action for you to take what you have learned and apply it not just in your day-to-day leadership roles but also in a broader context to drive positive change in your organization and community.

In conclusion, as you continue on your leadership journey, remember that each step you take builds on the last, and each challenge you overcome makes you a stronger, more effective leader. Keep pushing forward, keep learning, and keep leading with courage, integrity, and a vision for the betterment of those around you. Your journey continues, and the impact you can make is limitless.

Leadership Resources and Further Development

For anyone who is passionate about deepening their leadership skills and abilities, especially through tough periods, gathering resources and seeking further development opportunities can be the most proactive steps you can take, and this chapter is dedicated to guiding you through a variety of valuable resources that can enhance your leadership journey. When you think about improving your leadership abilities, it's not just about reading books or attending seminars; rather, it involves a continuous process of learning, practicing, and connecting with others who can provide insights and support, which is why this section provides a comprehensive listing of books, websites, and courses that have been carefully selected to help you grow as a leader. Furthermore, for those who seek a more personalized approach, this section also covers how you can access coaching or consultancy services, which are excellent ways to receive tailored advice and strategies that align with your specific leadership challenges and goals.

Developing a personal leadership plan is an actionable step that cannot be overlooked, and this chapter provides detailed guidelines on how to create one; such plans are vital as they serve as a roadmap for your development, helping you to identify areas for improvement, set achievable goals, and track your progress over time, ensuring that you are not only learning but also applying what you learn in a way that positively impacts your leadership capabilities. In addition, the importance of community and shared learning experiences is emphasized through suggestions for forming leadership study groups or engaging in mentoring relationships, which can be incredibly beneficial, as they offer a platform for exchanging ideas, receiving feedback, and learning from the experiences of others, thereby enriching your understanding and application of leadership concepts. These groups and relationships foster a supportive environment where leaders can challenge each other and grow together, making the journey of leadership development more engaging and effective.

When considering the resources mentioned, it's crucial to choose those that resonate with your personal leadership style and the specific challenges you face; every leader is unique, and what works for one might not work for another, so taking the time to assess each resource and how it can contribute to your growth is essential. The recommended readings cover a range of topics from strategic leadership to emotional intelligence, each providing unique perspectives and practical advice that can broaden your understanding of what effective leadership looks like and how it can be achieved, even during tough times. Websites and online courses offer flexible learning opportunities that can fit into your busy schedule, allowing you to learn at your own pace while still providing comprehensive content and interactive experiences that enhance your learning.

Lastly, the chapter discusses how you can engage with these resources effectively; it's not enough to simply read a book or complete a course, but rather, how you apply what you learn to your real-life leadership challenges that will ultimately determine the effectiveness of your learning. Engaging critically with the material, practicing the techniques discussed, and reflecting on your leadership practices are all

191

part of a holistic approach to leadership development. By actively engaging with these resources, you are taking significant steps toward not only understanding leadership on a deeper level but also enhancing your ability to lead effectively, no matter the challenges you may face.

In conclusion, this chapter serves as a comprehensive guide to selecting and utilizing a variety of leadership resources that can propel your development and help you navigate the complexities of leadership through challenging periods. By taking the initiative to explore and engage with these resources, you are committing to a path of continuous improvement and transformative leadership, which is essential for anyone looking to make a significant impact in their personal and professional life.

Resources To Help Shape Leadership Style

Managing a team of employees is no easy feat. Different styles of leadership yield different results, so it's important to understand which one suits you and your team best.

One great way to discover your own management style is by reading about leadership and business, and experimenting with different management resources. That's why we asked the members of Forbes Business Council which book or resource has been particularly helpful in shaping their management style. Below, 11 of them shared their favorites.

1. Principles

Reading Principles: Life and Work, by Ray Dalio, in large sections or even just a few passages can be a grounding reminder to keep yourself, your team and things in general in perspective. My personal favorite passage and life reminder is, "Make your passion and your work one and the same and do it with people you want to be with." – Kim DeLine, Elevate K-12

2. Delivering Happiness

Many business owners overlook the importance of the mental health of their employees. Tony Hsieh's Delivering Happiness: A Path to Profits, Passion, and Purpose influenced my management style because it emphasized the significance of office culture. Employee happiness directly impacts customer satisfaction, thus it was essential to establish an amazing culture where my team could be themselves and feel at home. – Sardor Umidinov, Home Alliance

Forbes Business Council is the foremost growth and networking organization for business owners and leaders. Do I qualify?

3. The Culture Code

The Culture Code: The Secrets of Highly Successful Groups, by Daniel Coyle, breaks down managerial myths that no longer work. As talent continues to be difficult for businesses to attract and retain, culture is the retention tool for building an unshakable foundation for growth. Modeling roles, promoting the right people and behaviors and creating safe environments to talk and share ideas are the solution to any business' talent conundrum. – Dandan Zhu, DG Recruit.

4. The 7 Habits of Highly Effective People

The 7 Habits of Highly Effective People, by Stephen R. Covey, is a great resource. The section on interdependence is especially influential in our internal management style. Think win-win, seek first to understand and synergize! We're big on teamwork and Covey's ideas are paramount. We keep things organized on Trello and we experiment with training platforms like Trainual. – Corey Lewis, 1AND1 Life.

5. The Ten Faces of Innovation

The Ten Faces of Innovation: IDEO's Strategies for Beating the Devil's Advocate and Driving Creativity Throughout Your OrganizationThe Ten Faces of Innovation talks about people, the roles they can play, the hats they can wear and the personas they can adapt. Tom Kelley shows how the organization can bring the human components of innovation to your organization's operational work. It's about developing the personas of your team to maximize its influence. – Jennifer Ty, Excell Home Care Inc.

6. Mindset

Building cohesion within your entire team and giving your staffers a unified focus and purpose inspires them to work together. It's all about having a growth-oriented mindset. Mindset: The New Psychology of Success, by Carol S. Dweck, Ph.D., is a great book that covers this topic and can help evolve your management style. – Beth Worthy, GMR Transcription Services, Inc.

7. The Art of Gathering

The Art of Gathering: How We Meet and Why It Matters, by Priya Parker, is a wonderful book that changed the way I approach meetings. Parker stresses the importance of making all gatherings memorable by mapping out their purpose beforehand. Since time is everyone's most valuable asset, her strategies are right on target and help ensure meetings are useful for everyone. – Jeanne Hardy, Creative Business Inc.

8. People Styles at Work

A strong manager has the ability to manage people of all work styles and get the most out of them. How do you engage the person who insists on lengthy discussions and analysis before making a decision? What about when they are at odds with their fast-charging, action-oriented teammate? People Styles at Work…And Beyond: Making Bad Relationships Good and Good Relationships Better, by Robert Bolton, has been an invaluable guide on how to effectively lead all kinds of people. – Christine Tao, Sounding Board, Inc

9. Jim Collins Books

Jim Collins has authored some really fantastic books for managers. In particular, Good to Great: Why Some Companies Make the Leap and Others Don't And the newer Built to Last: Successful Habits of

Visionary Companies provide great examples of how companies from diverse fields maintain excellence. Even though some of the companies discussed have failed to weather the current market (Circuit City), they still provide insight into what does and does not work for managing a team. – Andrew M. Smith, McRight-Smith Construction

10. Classic Leadership Books

Modern leaders listen, learn and innovate. Functional expertise can be earned, but character-building traits, like purpose, compassion, humility, perseverance, integrity and respect must be honed. My resources are Sun Tzu's The Art of War, Simon Sinek's Start With Why: How Great Leaders Inspire Everyone to Take Action, Jim Collins' Good to Great: Why Some Companies Make the Leap and Others Don't, Ben Horowitz's The Hard Thing About Hard Things: Building a Business When There Are No Easy Answers and Alfred's Lansing's Endurance: Shackleton's Incredible Voyage. – Daphne Liu, Softescu

11. Harvard Business Review

Reading the stories and articles available on Harvard Business Review has been extremely insightful by giving first hand experiences, solutions to problems and advice anyone can take and easily apply to personally and to the business. I highly recommend all entrepreneurs visit the site when they're in a pinch or looking for insight on problems they are having. – Hoda Mahmoodzadegan, BAKT Global

Empowering People To Have a LIVING Relationship With God. Expecting Great From God & Attempting Great For God. Don't Let Bad News Change Your Mind!

www.ingramcontent.com/pod-product-compliance
Lightning Source LLC
Chambersburg PA
CBHW051618120626
46551CB00014B/1851